PUSHKIN PRESS

"Gems of literary perfection... Such lucid, liquid prose" Simon Winchester

"Zweig's accumulated historical and cultural studies remain a body of achievement almost too impressive to take in" Clive James

"The perfect stocking-filler" *Philosophy Football*

STEFAN ZWEIG was born in 1881 in Vienna. Between the two world wars he was an international bestselling author, famed for his gripping novellas, such as *Letter from an Unknown Woman*, his colourful historical biographies of figures such as Mary Stuart and Marie Antoinette, and above all for his vivid historical miniatures, five of which are included in this book. First published in 1927, these miniatures have never been out of print in German, selling more than three million copies, making them Zweig's most popular work. In 1934, with the rise of Nazism, he left Austria. He eventually settled in Brazil, where in 1942 he and his wife were found dead in an apparent double suicide. Much of his work is available from Pushkin Press.

GENIUS AND DISCOVERY

—

FIVE HISTORICAL MINIATURES

—

STEFAN ZWEIG

PUSHKIN PRESS

LONDON

Pushkin Press
71–75 Shelton Street,
London WC2H 9JQ

Original text © Williams Verlag AG Zurich
English translation © Anthea Bell, 2013

'The Discovery of El Dorado' first published in German in *Sternstunden der Menschheit*, 1927.

'Flight into Immortality', 'The Resurrection of George Frideric Handel', 'The Genius of a Night', 'The First Word to Cross the Ocean' first published in German in *Sternstunden der Menschheit*, 1940 edition.

This translation first published by Pushkin Press in *Shooting Stars: Ten Historical Miniatures* in 2013

This edition first published in 2016

10 9 8 7 6 5 4 3 2 1

ISBN 978 1 782272 75 5

All rights reserved. No part of this publication may be reproduced, stored in a retrieval system or transmitted in any form or by any means, electronic, mechanical, photocopying, recording or otherwise, without prior permission in writing from Pushkin Press

Cover design/art direction by Darren Wall
Cover illustration by Stuart Daly
Set in Monotype Dante by Tetragon, London

Printed and bound by CPI Group (UK) Ltd, Croydon CR0 4YY

www.pushkinpress.com

CONTENTS

Foreword 7

Flight into Immortality 11

The Resurrection of George Frideric Handel 47

The Genius of a Night 81

The Discovery of El Dorado 109

The First Word to Cross the Ocean 125

FOREWORD

No artist is an artist through the entire twenty-four hours of his normal day; he succeeds in producing all that is essential, all that will last, only in a few, rare moments of inspiration. History itself, which we may admire as the greatest writer and actor of all time, is by no means always creative. Even in "God's mysterious workshop", as Goethe reverently calls historical knowledge, a great many indifferent and ordinary incidents happen. As everywhere in life and art, sublime moments that will never be forgotten are few and far between. As a chronicler, history generally does no more than arrange events link by link, indifferently and persistently, fact by fact in a gigantic chain reaching through the millennia, for all tension needs a time of preparation, every incident with any true significance has to develop. Millions of people in a nation are necessary for a single genius to arise, millions of tedious hours must pass before a truly historic shooting star of humanity appears in the sky.

But if artistic geniuses do arise, they will outlast their own time; if such a significant hour in the history of the world occurs, it will decide matters for decades and centuries yet to come. As the electricity of the entire atmosphere is discharged at the tip of a lightning conductor, an immeasurable wealth of events is then crammed together in a small span of time. What usually happens at a leisurely pace, in sequence and due order, is concentrated into a single moment that determines and establishes everything: a single *Yes*, a single *No*, a *Too Soon* or a *Too Late* makes that hour irrevocable for hundreds of generations while deciding the life of a single man or woman, of a nation, even the destiny of all humanity.

Such dramatically compressed and fateful hours, in which a decision outlasting time is made on a single day, in a single hour, often just in a minute, are rare in the life of an individual and rare in the course of history. In this book I am aiming to remember the hours of such shooting stars—I call them that because they outshine the past as brilliantly and steadfastly as stars outshine the night. They come from very different periods of time and very different parts of the world. In none of them have I tried to give a new colour or to intensify the intellectual truth of inner or outer events by means of my own invention. For in those sublime moments when they emerge, fully formed, history needs no helping hand. Where the muse of history is truly a poet and a dramatist, no mortal writer may try to outdo her.

FLIGHT INTO
IMMORTALITY

THE DISCOVERY OF
THE PACIFIC OCEAN

---

25 September 1513

A Ship Is Fitted Out

When he first returned from the newly discovered continent of America, Columbus had displayed countless treasures and curiosities on his triumphal procession through the crowded streets of Seville and Barcelona: human beings of a race hitherto unknown, with reddish skins; animals never seen before; colourful, screeching parrots; slow-moving tapirs; then strange plants and fruits that would soon find a new home in Europe—Indian corn, tobacco, the coconut. The rejoicing throng marvels at all these things, but the royal couple and their counsellors are excited above all by a few boxes and baskets containing gold. Columbus does not bring much gold back from the new Indies: a few pretty things that he has bartered with the natives, or stolen from them, a few small bars and several handfuls of loose grains, gold dust rather than solid gold—the whole of it at most enough to mint a few hundred ducats. But the inspired Columbus, who always fanatically believes whatever he wants to believe at any given time, and who has been so gloriously proved right about his sea route to India, boasts effusively and in all honesty that this is only a tiny foretaste. Reliable news, he adds, has reached him of gold mines of immeasurable extent on these new islands; only just below the surface, the precious metal, he says, lies under a thin layer of soil in many fields, and you can easily dig it out with an ordinary spade. Farther south, however, there are realms where the kings drink from golden goblets, and gold is worth less than lead at home in Spain. The ever-avaricious king listens, intoxicated to hear of this new Ophir that now belongs to him. No one yet knows Columbus and his sublime folly well enough to doubt his promises. A great fleet is fitted out at once for the second voyage, and now there is no need for recruiting officers and drummers to find men to join it. Word of the newly discovered Ophir, where you can pick up gold from the ground with your bare hands, sends all Spain mad; people come in their hundreds, their thousands to travel to El Dorado, the land of gold.

But what a dismal tidal wave of humanity is now cast up by greed from every city, every village, every hamlet. Not only do honourable noblemen arrive, wishing to gild their coats of arms, not only are there bold adventurers and brave soldiers; all the filthy scum of Spain is also washed up in Palos and Cádiz. There are branded thieves, highwaymen and footpads hoping to find a more profitable trade in the land of gold; there are debtors who want to escape their creditors and husbands hoping to get away from scolding wives; all the desperadoes and failures, branded criminals and men sought by the Alguacil justices volunteer for the fleet, a motley band of failures who are determined that they will make their fortunes at long last, in an instant too, and to that end are ready to commit any act of violence and any crime. They have told one another the fantasies of Columbus, repeating that in those lands you have only to thrust a spade into the ground to see nuggets of gold glinting up at you, and the prosperous among the emigrants hire servants and mules to carry large quantities of the precious metal away. Those who do not succeed in being taken on by the expedition find another way: never troubling to get the royal permission, coarse-grained adventurers fit out ships for themselves, in order to cross the ocean as fast as they can and get their hands on gold, gold, gold. And at a single stroke, Spain is rid of troublemakers and the most dangerous kind of rabble.

The Governor of Española (later San Domingo and Haiti) is horrified to see these uninvited guests overrunning the island entrusted to his care. Year after year the ships bring new freight and increasingly rough, unruly fellows. The newcomers, in turn, are bitterly disappointed. There is no sign of gold lying loose on the road, and not another grain of corn can be got out of the unfortunate native inhabitants on whom these brutes descend. So hordes of them wander around, intent on robbery, terrifying the unhappy Indios and the governor alike. The latter tries in vain to make them colonists by showing them where land may be had, giving them cattle, and indeed ample supplies of human cattle in the form of sixty to seventy native inhabitants as slaves to work for every one of them. But neither the high-born hidalgos nor the former footpads have a mind to set up as farmers. They didn't come here to grow wheat and herd cattle; instead of putting their minds to sowing seed and harvesting crops, they torment the unfortunate Indios—they will have eradicated the entire indigenous population within a few years—or sit around in taverns. Within a short time most of them are so deep in debt that after their goods they have to sell their hats and coats, their last shirts, and they fall into the clutches of traders and usurers.

So in 1510 all these failures on Española are glad to hear that a well-regarded man from the island, the *bachiller* or lawyer Martín Fernandez de Enciso, is fitting out a ship with a new crew to come to the aid of his colony on terra firma. In 1509 two famous adventurers, Alonzo de Ojeda and Diego de

Nicuesa, received the privilege from King Ferdinand of founding a colony near the straits of Panama and the coast of Venezuela, naming it rather too hastily Castilla del Oro, Golden Castile. Intoxicated by the resonant name and beguiled by tall stories, the lawyer, who knew little about the ways of the world, had put most of his fortune into this adventure. But now no gold comes from the newly founded colony in San Sebastián on the Gulf of Urabá, only shrill cries for help. Half the crew have been killed in fighting the native people, and the other half have starved to death. To save the investment he has already made, Enciso ventures the rest of his fortune, and equips another expedition to go to the aid of the original one. As soon as they hear that Enciso needs soldiers, all the desperadoes and loafers on Española exploit this opportunity and take ship with him. Their aim is simply to get away, away from their creditors and the watchful eyes of the stern governor. But the creditors are also on their guard. They realize that the worst of their debtors intend to disappear, never to be seen again, and so they besiege the governor with requests to let no one travel without his special permission. The governor grants their wish. A strict guard obliges Enciso's ship to stay outside the harbour, while government boats patrol the coastal waters to prevent anyone without such permission from being smuggled aboard. And all the embittered desperadoes, who fear death less than honest work or their towering debts, watch as Enciso's ship leaves on its venture with all sail set.

The Man in the Crate

And so, with all sail set, Enciso's ship leaves Española and steers towards the American mainland. The outlines of the island it has left behind are already merging with the blue horizon. It is a calm voyage, and there is nothing in particular to be said about its early stages, or at most we may note that a huge and extremely powerful bloodhound—a son of the famous Becericco, who has become famous himself under the name of Leoncico—prowls restlessly up and down the deck, sniffing around everywhere. No one knows who owns the mighty animal or how he came on board. Finally the crew notice that the dog cannot be prised away from a particularly large crate of provisions that was brought aboard at the last minute. But lo and behold, this crate unexpectedly opens of its own accord, and out climbs a man of about thirty-five, well armed with sword, helmet and shield like Santiago, the patron saint of Castile. He is Vasco Núñez de Balboa, giving us the first evidence of his astonishing boldness and resource. Born in Jerez de los Caballeros of a noble family, he had sailed for the New World with Rodrigo de Bastidas as a private soldier and finally, after many wanderings, was stranded off Española along with his ship. The governor had tried in vain to make Núñez de Balboa into a good colonist; after a few months he had abandoned his allotted parcel of land and was bankrupt, and at a loss for a way to escape his creditors. But while the other debtors, clenching their fists, stare from the beach at the government boats that prevent them from getting away on Enciso's ship, Núñez de Balboa circumvents Diego Columbus's cordon by hiding in an empty provisions crate and getting accomplices to carry him aboard, where no one notices his cunning trick in all the tumult of putting out to sea. Only when he knows the ship is so far from the coast that the crew are unlikely to sail back to Española on his account does the stowaway emerge, and now here he is.

The *bachiller* Enciso is a man of law, and like lawyers in general has little romanticism in his soul. As Alcalde, chief of police in the new colony, he does not intend to put up with dubious characters. He brusquely informs Núñez de Balboa that he is not going to have him on his ship, but will put him ashore on the beach of the next island they pass, whether or not it is inhabited.

However, it never comes to that. For even as the ship is making for Castilla del Oro it meets—miraculously, in a time when only a few dozen vessels in all sail these still-unfamiliar seas—a heavily manned boat under a commander whose name will soon echo through the world, Francisco Pizarro. The men in the boat are from Enciso's colony of San Sebastián, and at first they are taken for mutineers who have left their posts of their own accord. But to Enciso's horror, they tell him there is no San Sebastián left, they themselves are the former colonists, their commander Ojeda has made off with one ship, the rest, who had only two brigantines, had to wait until all but seventy colonists had died before they could find room for themselves in the two small boats. One of those brigantines has been wrecked in its own turn; Pizarro's thirty-five men are the last survivors of Castilla del Oro. So now where are they to go? After hearing Pizarro's tale, Enciso's men have no taste for braving the swamp-like climate and the natives' poison-tipped arrows in the abandoned settlement; turning back to Española seems to them the only option. At this dangerous moment, Vasco Núñez de Balboa suddenly steps forward. He explains that after going on his first voyage with Rodrigo de Bastidas, he knows the whole coast of Central America, and he remembers that at the time of that voyage they found a place called Darién on the bank of a gold-bearing river where the natives were friendly. They should found the new settlement there, he suggests, not in this unhappy place.

At once the whole crew comes down on Núñez de Balboa's side. In line with his proposition, they steer for Darién on the Panama isthmus, where they first indulge in the usual slaughter of the natives, and as some gold is found among the goods they rob, the desperadoes decide to found a settlement here, in pious gratitude naming the new town Santa María de la Antigua del Darién.

A Dangerous Rise

The unfortunate financier of the colony, the *bachiller* Enciso, will soon be sorry he did not throw the crate overboard with Núñez de Balboa inside it, for after a few weeks that audacious man has all the power in his hands. As a lawyer who grew up believing in order and discipline, Enciso tries to administer the colony on behalf of the Spanish Crown in his capacity as Alcalde, the chief of police of the governor, who cannot be found just now, and enacts his edicts as sternly in the wretched huts of the Indios as if he were sitting in his legal chambers in Seville. In the middle of this wilderness where no humans have ever trod before, he forbids the soldiers to haggle over gold with the natives, gold being reserved for the Crown; he tries to force this undisciplined rabble to observe law and order, but the adventurers instinctively back a man of the sword rather than a man of the pen. Soon Balboa is the real master of the colony; Enciso has to flee to save his life, and when Nicuesa, one of the governors appointed to the mainland by the king, finally arrives to enforce the law Balboa refuses to let him land. The unhappy Nicuesa, hunted out of the land allotted to him by the king, drowns on the voyage back.

So now Núñez de Balboa, the man from the crate, lords it over the colony. But in spite of his success he does not feel very comfortable about it. He has openly rebelled against the king, and can hardly hope for pardon because it is his fault that the appointed governor is dead. He knows that Enciso, who has fled, is on his way to Spain with his complaints, and sooner or later he, Balboa, will be brought to trial for his rebellion. All the same, Spain is far away, and he has plenty of time left, all the time it takes for a ship to cross the ocean twice. Being as clever as he is bold, he looks for the only way to hold the power he has usurped for as long as possible. He knows that at this time success justifies all crimes, and a large delivery of gold to the royal treasury may well moderate or delay any punishment. So first he must lay hands on gold, for gold is power! Together with Francisco Pizarro, he subjugates and robs the indigenous people of the vicinity, and in the midst of the usual slaughter he achieves a crucial success. One of the natives, Careta by name, suggests that as he is already likely to die he might prefer not to make enemies of the Indios, and instead conclude an alliance with Careta's own tribe, offering him his daughter's hand as a pledge of his own good faith. Núñez de Balboa immediately recognizes the importance of having a reliable and powerful friend among the natives; he accepts Careta's offer, and—what is even more surprising—he remains an affectionate lover of the Indian girl until his last hour. Together with Careta he defeats all the local Indios, and acquires such authority among them that in the end the mightiest of their chieftains, Comagre by name, respectfully invites him to his home.

This visit to the powerful Indio chief ushers in a decision of great importance to international history as well as to the life of Vasco Núñez de Balboa, who has hitherto been only a desperado and bold rebel against the Crown of Spain, destined by the law courts of Castile to die by the axe or the noose. Comagre receives him in a stone house with spacious rooms, a dwelling that astonishes Vasco Núñez by the wealth of its furnishings; and, unasked, the chieftain makes his guest a present of 4,000 ounces of gold. And now it is Comagre's turn to be astonished, for as soon as the Sons of Heaven, the mighty and godlike strangers whom he has received with such reverence, set eyes on the gold there is an end to their dignity. Like dogs let off the chain they attack one another, swords are drawn, fists clenched, they shout and rage, every man wants his own share of the gold. The Indio chief watches the disorder in scornful surprise; his is the eternal amazement of children of nature the world over at those cultured people to whom a handful of yellow metal appears more precious than all the intellectual and technical achievements of their civilization.

At last the native chief addresses them, and with a shiver of greed the Spaniards hear what the interpreter translates. How strange, says Comagre, that you quarrel with each other over such small things, that you expose your lives to the utmost discomfort and danger for the sake of such a common metal. Over there, beyond those mountains, lies a huge lake, and all the rivers that flow into it bring gold down with them. A people live there who have ships like yours, with sails and oars, and their kings eat and drink from golden vessels. You can find as much of this yellow metal there as you want. It is a dangerous journey, for the chieftains on the way will certainly refuse to let you pass, but it would take only a few days.

Vasco Núñez de Balboa feels his heart contract. At last he is on the track of the legendary land of gold, the land that they have dreamt of for years and years; his predecessors have hoped for a sight of it in the south and the north, and now, if this native is telling the truth, it lies only a few days' journey away. And at the same time he had proof of the existence of that other ocean to which Columbus, Cabot, Corte-Real, all those great and famous seafarers, have sought the way in vain, and the way around the globe is discovered too. The name of the man who is first to see that new sea and take possession of it for his motherland will never perish on this earth. Now Balboa knows what he must do to absolve himself of all blame and win everlasting honour: he must be first to cross the isthmus to the Mar del Sur, the southern sea that is the way to India, and conquer this new Ophir for the Spanish Crown. That hour in the chief Comagre's house has determined his fate. From now on, the life of this chance-come adventurer has a higher meaning, one that will outlast time.

Flight into Immortality

There can be no greater happiness in the life of a man than to have discovered his life's purpose in the middle of its span, in his years of creativity. Núñez de Balboa knows what is at stake for him—either a pitiful death on the scaffold or immortality. First he must buy peace with the Crown, in retrospect legitimizing and legalizing his crime when he usurped power! So the rebel of yesterday, now the most zealous of subjects, sends Pasamonte, the royal treasurer on Española, not only the one-fifth of Comagre's gift of gold that belongs to the Crown by law, but as he is better versed in the practices of the world than that dry lawyer Enciso he adds to the official consignment a private financial donation to the treasurer, asking to be confirmed in his office as Captain-General of the colony. In fact Pasamonte the treasurer has no authority to do so, but in return for the gold he sends Núñez de Balboa a provisional, if in truth worthless, document. At the same time Balboa, wishing to secure himself on all sides, has also sent two of his most reliable men to Spain to tell the court about all he has done for the Crown, conveying the important information that he has induced the Indio chieftain to support him. He needs, Vasco Núñez de Balboa tells the authorities in Seville, only a troop of 1,000 men, and with those men he will undertake to do more for Castile than any other Spaniard before him. He engages to discover the new sea and gain possession of the Land of Gold, now located at long last, the land promised by Columbus that never materialized but that he, Balboa, will conquer.

Everything now seems to have turned out well for the man who was once a rebel and a desperado. But the next ship from Spain brings bad news. One of his accomplices, a man whom he sent over to defuse the complaints at court of the robbed Enciso, tells him that such a mission is dangerous for him, even mortally dangerous. The cheated *bachiller* has gone to the Spanish law courts with his accusation of the man who robbed him of his power, and Balboa must pay him compensation. Meanwhile, the news of the nearby southern sea, which might have saved him, has not arrived yet; in any case, the next ship to cross the ocean will bring a lawyer to call Balboa to account for the trouble he has caused, and either judge him on the spot or take him back to Spain in chains.

Vasco Núñez de Balboa realizes that he is lost. He has been condemned before his message about the nearby southern sea and the Golden Coast arrives. Naturally news of it will be exploited even as his head rolls into the sand—someone else will bring his deed to completion, the great deed that he dreamt of. He himself can hope for nothing more from Spain. They know there that he hounded the king's rightful governor to his death, that he personally drove the Alcalde out of office—he will have to consider the verdict merciful if it is merely imprisonment, and he does not have to pay for his deeds on the block. He cannot count on powerful friends, for he has no power of his own left, and his best advocate, the gold, has too soft a voice to ensure mercy for him. Only one thing can save him now from the punishment for his audacity, and that is even greater audacity. If he discovers the other sea and the new Ophir before the lawyers arrive, and their henchmen take him and put him in fetters, he can save himself. Only one kind of flight is open to him here at the end of the inhabited world: flight into a great achievement, into immortality.

So Núñez de Balboa decides not to wait for the 1,000 men he asked Spain to send for the conquest of the unknown ocean, still less for the arrival of the lawyers. Better to venture on a monstrous deed with a few like-minded men! Better to die honourably for one of the boldest ventures of all times than be dragged shamefully to the scaffold with his hands bound. Núñez de Balboa calls the colony together, explains, without concealing the difficulties, his intention of crossing the isthmus, and asks who will follow him. His courage puts fresh heart into the others. A hundred and ninety soldiers, almost the entire defensive force of the colony capable of bearing arms, volunteer. There is not much equipment to be found, for these men are already living in a state of constant warfare. And on 1st September 1513 Núñez de Balboa, hero and bandit, adventurer and rebel, intent on escaping the gallows or a dungeon, sets out on his march into immortality.

An Immortal Moment

They begin to cross the isthmus in the province of Coyba, the little realm of the chief Careta whose daughter is Balboa's companion; it will later turn out that Núñez de Balboa has not chosen the narrowest place, in his ignorance thus extending the dangerous crossing by several days. But for such a bold venture into the unknown, his main concern is to have the security of a friendly Indian tribe, for support or in the case of a withdrawal. His men cross from Darién to Coyba in ten large canoes, 190 soldiers armed with spears, swords, arquebuses and crossbows, accompanied by a pack of the much-feared bloodhounds. His ally the Indian chief provides Indios to act as guides and bearers, and on 6th September the famous march across the isthmus begins, a venture making enormous demands on the will-power of those tried and tested adventurers. The Spanish first have to cross the low-lying areas in stifling equatorial heat that saps their strength; the marshy ground, full of feverish infections, was to kill many thousands of men working on the building of the Panama Canal centuries later. From the first they have to hack their way through the untrodden, poisonous jungle of creepers with axes and swords. The first of the troop, as if working inside a huge green mine, cut a narrow tunnel through the undergrowth for the others, and the army of conquistadors then strides along in single file, an endlessly long line of men, always with weapons in their hands, on the alert both day and night to repel any sudden attack by the native Indios. The heat is stifling in the sultry, misty darkness of the moist vault of giant trees as a pitiless sun blazes down above them. Drenched in sweat and with parched lips, the heavily armed men drag themselves on, mile after mile. Sometimes sudden downpours of rain fall like a hurricane, little streams instantly become torrential rivers, and the men have to either wade through them or cross them over swaying bridges improvised from palm fibres by the Indios. The Spanish have nothing to eat but a handful of maize; weary with lack of sleep, hungry, thirsty, surrounded by myriads of stinging, blood-sucking insects, they work their way forward in garments torn by thorns, footsore, their eyes feverish, their cheeks swollen by the stings of the whirring midges, restless by day, sleepless by night, and soon they are entirely exhausted. Even after the first week of marching, a large part of the troop can no longer stand up to the stress, and

Núñez de Balboa, who knows that the real danger still lies in wait for them, gives orders for all those sick with fever and worn out to stay behind. He means to brave the crucial venture only with the best of his troop.

At last the ground begins to rise. The jungle becomes less dense now that its full tropical luxuriance can unfold only in the marshy hollows. But when there is no shade to protect them, the equatorial sun high overhead, glaring and hot, beats down on their heavy armour. Slowly and by short stages, the weary men manage to climb the hilly country to the mountain chain that separates the narrow stretch of land between the two oceans like a stone backbone. Gradually the view is freer, and the air is refreshing by night. After eighteen days of heroic effort, they seem to have overcome the worst difficulty; already the crest of the mountain range rises before them, and from the peaks, so the Indian guides say, they will be able to see both oceans, the Atlantic and the still-unknown and unnamed Pacific. But now of all times, just when they seem to have overcome the tough, vicious resistance of nature, they face a new enemy: the native chieftain of that province, who bars the strangers' way with hundreds of his warriors. Núñez de Balboa has plenty of experience of fighting off the Indios. All he has to do is get the men to fire a salvo from their arquebuses, and that artificial thunder and lightning exerts its proven magical power once again over the local population. Screaming, the terrified warriors run, the Spanish and their bloodhounds in pursuit. Instead of enjoying this easy victory, however, Balboa, like all the Spanish conquistadors, dishonours it by terrible cruelty, having a number of defenceless, bound prisoners torn apart alive by the hungry dogs, their flesh reduced to scraps, a spectacle staged as a substitute for bullfights and gladiatorial games. Dreadful slaughter shames the last night before Núñez de Balboa's immortal day.

There is a unique, inexplicable mixture in the character and manner of these Spanish conquistadors. Pious believers as ever any Christians were, they call upon God from the ardent depths of their souls, at the same time committing the most shocking inhumanities of history in his name. Capable of the most magnificent and heroic feats of courage, sacrifice and suffering, they still deceive and fight one another shamelessly; yet in the midst of their contemptible behaviour they have a strong feeling of honour, and a wonderful, indeed truly admirable sense of the historic importance of their mission. That same Núñez de Balboa who threw innocent, bound and defenceless prisoners to the bloodthirsty dogs the evening before, perhaps caressing the jaws of the animals in satisfaction while they were still dripping with human blood, understands the precise significance of his deed in the story of mankind, and at the crucial moment finds one of those great gestures that remain unforgettable over the ages. He knows that this day, the 25th of September, will be remembered in the history of the world, and with true Spanish feeling the hard, thoughtless adventurer lets it be known how fully he has grasped the lasting gravity of his mission.

Balboa's gesture is this: that evening, directly after the bloodbath, one of the natives has pointed out a nearby peak, telling him that from its height you can see the other ocean, the unknown Mar del Sur. Immediately Balboa makes his arrangements. Leaving the injured and exhausted men in the plundered village, he orders those still capable of marching—sixty-seven of them in all, out of the original 190 with whom he began the expedition in Darién—to climb the mountain. They approach the peak at ten in the morning. There is only a small, bare hilltop yet to be scaled, and then the view must stretch out before their eyes.

At this moment Balboa commands his men to stop. None of them is to follow him, for he does not want to share this first sight of the new ocean with anyone else. After crossing one gigantic ocean in our world, the Atlantic, he alone will be, now and for ever, the first Spaniard, the first European, the first Christian to set eyes on the still-unknown other ocean, the Pacific. Slowly, with his heart thudding, deeply aware of the significance of the moment, he climbs on, a flag in his left hand, his sword in his right hand, a solitary silhouette in the vast orb. Slowly he scales the hilltop, without haste, for the real work has already been done. Only a few more steps, fewer now, still fewer, and once he has reached the peak a great view opens up before him. Beyond the mountains, wooded and green as the hills descend below him, lies an endless expanse of water with reflections as of metal in it: the sea, the new and unknown sea, hitherto only dreamt of and never seen, the legendary sea sought in vain by Columbus and all who came after him, the ocean whose waves lap against the shores of America, India and China. And Vasco Núñez de Balboa looks and looks and looks, blissfully proud as he drinks in the knowledge that his are the first European eyes in which the endless blue of that ocean is mirrored.

Vasco Núñez de Balboa gazes long and ecstatically into the distance. Only then does he call up his comrades to share his joy and pride. Restless and excited, gasping for breath and crying out aloud, they scramble, climb and run up the last hill, they stare in amazement and gaze with astonishment in their eyes. All of a sudden Father Anselm de Vara, who is with the party, strikes up the *Te Deum laudamus*, and at once all the noise and shouting dies down, all the harsh, rough voices of those soldiers, adventurers and bandits uniting in the devout hymn. The Indios watch in astonishment as, at a word from the priest, they cut down a tree to erect a cross, carving the initials of the King of Spain's name in the wood. And when the cross rises, it is as if its two wooden arms were reaching out to both seas, the Atlantic and the Pacific Oceans, and all the hidden distance beyond them.

In the midst of the awed silence, Núñez de Balboa steps forward and addresses his soldiers. They did right, he says, to thank God who of his grace has granted them such honour, and pray to him to continue helping them to conquer that sea and all these lands. If they will continue following him faithfully, he adds, they will go home from these new Indies the richest Spaniards ever known. He solemnly raises his flag to all four winds, to take possession on behalf of Spain of all the distant lands where those winds blow. Then he calls the clerk, Andrés de Valderrabáno, telling him to write out a certificate recording this solemn act for all time to come. Andrés de Valderrabáno unrolls a parchment that he has carried in a closed wooden container with an inkwell and a quill all the way through the jungle, and commands all the noblemen and knights and men-at-arms—*los caballeros e hidalgos y hombres de bien*—"who were present at the discovery of the southern sea, the Mar del Sur, by the noble and highly honoured Captain Vasco Núñez de Balboa, His Majesty's Governor", to confirm that "this Master Vasco Núñez de Balboa was the man who first set eyes on that sea and showed it to his followers".

Then the sixty-seven men climbed down the hill, and since that day, the 25th of September 1513, mankind has known of the last and hitherto undiscovered ocean on earth.

Gold and Pearls

At last they are certain of it. They have seen the sea. And now to go down to its coast, feel the flowing water, touch it, taste it, pick up flotsam and jetsam from the beach! It takes them two days to climb down, and so that in future he will know the quickest way from the mountain range to the sea, Núñez de Balboa divides his men into separate groups. The third of these groups, under Alonzo Martín, is the first to arrive on the beach, and even the simple soldiers of this group of adventurers are so full of the vanity of fame, so thirsty for immortality, that Alonzo Martín himself, a plain, straightforward man, instantly gets the clerk to write down in black and white that he was the first to plunge his foot and his hand in those still-unnamed waters. Only after he has exchanged his small ego for a mote of immortality does he let Balboa know that he has reached the sea and felt its water with his own hand. Balboa immediately prepares for another grand gesture. Next day, Michaelmas Day by the calendar, he appears with only twenty-two companions on the beach, armed and girded like St Michael himself, to take possession of the new sea in a solemn ceremony. He does not stride into the water at once, but waits haughtily like its lord and master, resting under a tree until the rising tide sends a wave washing up to him, licking around his feet like an obedient dog. Only then does he stand up, slinging his shield on his back so that it gleams like a mirror in the sun, take his sword in one hand and in the other the flag of Castile bearing the portrait of the Virgin Mary, and stride into the water. Not until he is deep in those vast, strange waters, the waves breaking round his waist, does Núñez de Balboa, once a rebel and desperado, now the faithful servant and triumphant general of his king, wave the flag on all sides, crying in a loud voice: "Long live those high and mighty monarchs Ferdinand and Joanna of Castile, León and Aragón, in whose names and in favour of the royal Crown of Castile I take true, physical and lasting possession of all these seas and lands, coasts and harbours and islands, and I swear that should any prince or any other captain, Christian or heathen or of any other faith or rank whatsoever, lay claim to these lands and seas I will defend them in the name of the kings of Castile, whose property they are, now and for all time, as long as the world shall last and until the Day of Judgement."

All the Spaniards repeat this oath, and for a moment their words drown out the roaring of the waves. Each man moistens his lips with seawater, and once again the clerk Andrés de Valderrabáno takes note of this act of possession, closing his document with the words: "These twenty-two men, as well as the clerk Andrés de Valderrabáno, were the first Christians to set foot in the Mar del Sur, and they all tried the water with their hands, and moistened their mouths with it, to see whether it was salt water like the water of the other sea. And when they saw that it was so they gave thanks to God."

The great deed is done. Now they have yet to derive earthly benefit from their heroic undertaking. The Spanish plunder or barter a little gold with some of the natives. But a new surprise awaits them in the midst of their triumph, for the Indios bring them whole handfuls of the precious pearls that are to be found on the neighbouring islands in rich profusion, including one, known as La Pellegrina, celebrated by Cervantes and Lope de Vega because, as one of the loveliest of all pearls, it adorned the royal crown of Spain and England. The Spaniards stuff all their pockets and sacks full of these precious things, which are not worth much more here than shells and sand, and when they greedily ask about what, to them, is the most important thing in the world—gold—one of the natives points south, to where the line of the mountains blurs softly into the horizon. There, he explains, lies a land of untold treasure, its rulers dine off golden vessels, and large four-legged animals—he means llamas—drag the most wonderful of loads into the king's treasury. And he tells them the name of the country that lies south in the sea and beyond the mountains. It is something like *Birù*, a strange and melodious sound.

Vasco Núñez de Balboa stares the way the man's hand is pointing, into the distance where the mountains disappear in the pallor of the sky. That soft and seductive word, *Birù*, has written itself at once on his soul. His heart thuds restlessly. For the second time in his life, he has found great, unhoped-for promise. The first message, Comagre's information about the nearby sea, has proved true. He has found the beach of pearls and the Mar del Sur. Perhaps the second message will be the same; perhaps he will succeed in discovering and conquering the Inca domain, the golden land of this earth.

The Gods Grant only
One Immortal Deed

Núñez de Balboa is still staring into the distance with a longing gaze. The word *Birù*, "Peru", rings in his mind like a golden bell. But he knows—with painful resignation—that he cannot venture to find out more this time. You cannot conquer a kingdom with two or three dozen worn-out men. So first he must go back to Darién, and later, with all the forces he can gather, set out on the way he has now discovered to find the new Ophir. But the march back is as hard as the march out to find the ocean. Once again the Spaniards must fight their way through the jungle, once again they must repel attacks by the natives. And they are not a fighting unit now, but a small group of men sick with fever and staggering with the last of their strength—Balboa himself is near death, and has to be carried in a hammock by the Indios. After four months of terrible stress and strain, he gets back to Darién on 19th January 1514. But one of the great deeds of history has been done. Balboa has fulfilled his promise, all who ventured into the unknown with him are rich now; his soldiers have brought home from the coast of the southern sea treasures never known to Columbus and the other conquistadors, and all the other colonists get their share. One-fifth is put aside for the Crown, and no one begrudges the conqueror the fact that he treats his dog Leoncico like any other warrior as a reward for tearing the flesh from the bones of the unhappy natives, and presents him with 500 gold pesos. Not a man in the colony now quarrels with Balboa's authority as governor after such an achievement. The adventurer and rebel is honoured like a god, and he can prepare with pride to send Spain the news that he has performed the greatest deed for the Crown of Castile since Columbus. The sun of his good fortune, rising steeply, has broken through all the clouds that have loomed over his life until now. It is at its zenith.

But Balboa's happiness does not last long. On a radiant June day a few months later the astonished people of Darién flock down to the beach. A sail has been sighted on the horizon, and already it is like a miracle in this forsaken corner of the world. And look, a second sail appears beside it, a third, a fourth, a fifth; and soon there are ten, no, fifteen, no, twenty—a whole fleet making for the harbour. Soon everyone knows: all this is the work of Núñez de Balboa's letter, but not the letter with the news of his triumph—which has not yet reached Spain—but the earlier letter in which, for the first time, he described the native chief's account of the nearby southern sea and the land of gold, asking for an army of 1,000 men to conquer those lands. The Spanish Crown did not hesitate to equip such a mighty fleet for that expedition, but no one in Seville and Barcelona thought of entrusting so important a task to a rebellious adventurer with such a bad reputation as Vasco Núñez de Balboa. Their own choice of governor is sent. A rich, aristocratic and highly regarded man of sixty, Pedro Arias Dávila, usually called Pedrarias, comes with the fleet to act as the king's governor and restore order to the colony at last, do justice for all the crimes so far committed, find the southern sea and conquer the promised land of gold.

The situation is an awkward one for Pedrarias. On the one hand he has the mission of calling the rebel Núñez de Balboa to account for his earlier hunting-down of the first governor, and if he is proved guilty putting him in chains or executing him; on the other, he has to discover the southern sea. However, as soon as his boat comes ashore he learns that this same Núñez de Balboa, whom he is to bring to justice, has done the great deed himself, that the rebel has already celebrated the triumph meant for him, and has done the Spanish Crown the greatest service since the discovery of America. Of course he cannot now put such a man's head on the block as if he were a common criminal; he must greet him courteously and offer honest congratulations.

From this moment, however, Núñez de Balboa is lost. Pedrarias will never forgive his rival for having done the deed that he himself was to do, and that would have ensured his eternal fame through the ages. Of course, he must hide his hatred for their hero from the colonists for fear of embittering them too soon; the investigation is adjourned, and Pedrarias even makes a show of peace by betrothing his own daughter, whom he has left in Spain, to Núñez de Balboa. But his hatred and jealousy of Balboa are in no way mollified, only heightened when a decree arrives from Spain, where they have at last heard of Balboa's deed, bestowing a suitable title on the former rebel making him an Adelantado, and telling Pedrarias to consult him on every important matter. This country is too small for two governors; one will have to give way, one of the two must go under. Vasco Núñez de Balboa senses that the sword hangs over him, for military and legal power are in the hands of Pedrarias. So for a second time he tries flight, which served him so well the first time, flight into immortality. He asks Pedrarias for permission to equip an expedition to explore the coast of the southern sea and conquer the land for a long way around. But the former rebel's secret intention is to make himself independent of any control on the other side of the sea, build his own fleet, be master of his own province and if possible also conquer the legendary Birù, that Ophir of the New World. Pedrarias cunningly agrees. If Balboa perishes in the attempt, all the better. If he succeeds, there will still be time to get rid of that over-ambitious man.

So Núñez de Balboa embarks upon his new flight into immortality, and the second is perhaps yet more magnificent than the first, even if the same fame has not been allotted to it in history, which honours only success. This time Balboa does not cross the isthmus only with his men. He has the wood, planks, sails, anchors and pulleys to build four brigantines dragged over the mountains by thousands of natives. Once he has a fleet over there, he can take possession of all the coasts, conquer the pearl islands and the legendary land of Peru. This time, however, fate is against the adventurer, and he keeps encountering new resistance. On his march through the moist jungle worms eat the wood, the planks rot and are useless. Not to be discouraged, Balboa has more trees cut down and fresh planks prepared on the Gulf of Panama. His energy performs true wonders—all seems to be going well, the brigantines are already built, the first in the Pacific Ocean. Then a sudden tornado floods the rivers where the ships lie ready. They are torn away and capsize in the sea. Balboa must begin again for the third time, and now at last he manages to complete two brigantines. Only two more, three more are needed now, and then he can set off and conquer the land of which he dreams day and night, ever since that native pointed south with his outstretched hand, and he heard, for the first time, the tempting name Birù. Recruit a few brave officers and good reinforcements for his crews, and he can found his realm! Only a few more months, only a little luck to go with his innate daring, and the name of the conqueror of the Incas would be known to world history not as Pizarro, the conqueror of Peru, but as Núñez de Balboa.

Even to its favourites, however, fate is not always generous. The gods seldom grant mortal man more than a single immortal deed.

Downfall

With iron-hard energy, Núñez de Balboa has prepared his great enterprise. But the success of his audacity in itself puts him in danger, for the suspicious eyes of Pedrarias anxiously observe his subordinate's intentions. Perhaps news has reached him, through treachery, of Balboa's ambitions to rule his own province; perhaps it is just that he jealously fears a second success on the part of the former rebel. At all events, he suddenly sends Balboa a very friendly letter, asking him to come back to Acla, a town near Darién, for a discussion before he sets out on his voyage of conquest. Balboa, hoping to get more support from Pedrarias in the form of reinforcements, accepts the invitation and immediately turns back. Outside the gates of the town, a small troop of soldiers marches towards him, apparently to greet him; he joyfully goes to meet the men and to embrace their leader, his brother-in-arms of many years, his companion in the discovery of the southern sea, his great friend Francisco Pizarro.

But Pizarro lays a heavy hand on his shoulder and tells him he is under arrest. Pizarro too longs for immortality, he too longs to conquer the land of gold, and perhaps he is not sorry to know that so bold a predecessor will be out of the way. Pedrarias the governor opens the trial for alleged rebellion, and it goes ahead fast and in defiance of justice. A few days later Vasco Núñez de Balboa and the most loyal of his companions go to the block. The executioner's sword flashes, and in a second, as his head rolls, the first human eyes ever to see both the oceans that embrace our earth at the same time are extinguished for ever.

THE RESURRECTION OF
GEORGE FRIDERIC HANDEL

21 August 1741

O N THE AFTERNOON of 13th April 1737 George Frideric Handel's manservant was sitting at the ground-floor window of the house in Brook Street, very strangely occupied. He had found, to his annoyance, that his supply of tobacco had run out, and in fact he had only to go a couple of streets away to buy more at his sweetheart Dolly's shop, but he dared not leave the house for fear of his lord and master, a hot-tempered man. George Frideric Handel had come home from rehearsal in a towering rage, his face bright red from the blood that had risen to it, the veins standing out like thick cords at his temples. He had slammed the front door of the house and now, as the servant could hear, he was marching up and down on the first floor so vigorously that the ceiling shook; it was unwise to be negligent in his service on days when he was in such a fury.

So the servant was seeking diversion from his boredom by puffing not elegant rings of blue smoke from his short clay pipe, but soap bubbles. He had mixed a little bowl of soapsuds and was amusing himself by blowing the brightly coloured bubbles out of the window and into the street. Passers-by stopped, bursting a bubble here and there with their canes in jest, they laughed and waved, but they showed no surprise. For anything might be expected of this house in Brook Street; the harpsichord might suddenly play loud music by night, you might hear prima donnas weeping and sobbing as the choleric German, falling into a berserk rage, uttered threats against them for singing an eighth of a tone too high or too low. The neighbours in Grosvenor Square had long considered Number 25 Brook Street a madhouse.

The servant blew his bright bubbles silently and persistently. After a while his skills visibly improved; the marbled bubbles grew ever larger and more thin-skinned, they rose higher and higher, floating more lightly through the air, and one even sailed over the low roof ridge of the house opposite. Then he suddenly gave a start of alarm, for a dull thud made the whole house shake. Glasses clinked, curtains swayed; something massive and heavy must have fallen on the floor above. The manservant jumped up and raced upstairs to the study.

The armchair in which his master sat to work was empty, the room itself was empty, and the servant was about to hurry into the bedroom when he saw

THE RESURRECTION OF GEORGE FRIDERIC HANDEL

Handel lying motionless on the floor, his eyes open and staring; and now, as the servant stood stock still in his initial panic, he heard heavy, stertorous breathing. The strong man was lying on his back groaning, or rather the groans were forcing their way out of him in short and increasingly weak grunts.

He's dying, thought the frightened servant, and he quickly knelt down to help the semi-conscious Handel. He tried to raise him and carry him to the sofa, but the huge man's body was too heavy, too great a burden. So he simply loosened the neckcloth constricting Handel's throat, and the stertorous breathing at once died away.

And now up from the floor below came Christof Schmidt, the master's secretary and assistant, who had just been copying out some arias. He too had been alarmed by the heavy fall. The two of them raised the weight of the man—his arms dangled limp, like the arms of a dead corpse—and laid him on the sofa with his head raised. "Undress him," Schmidt ordered the servant. "I'll run for the doctor. And splash water on him until he comes round."

Christof Schmidt ran out without his coat, wasting no time, and hurried down Brook Street towards Bond Street, waving to all the coaches that trotted sedately by and took no notice at all of the stout, panting man in his shirtsleeves. At last one of them stopped. Lord Chandos's coachman had recognized

Schmidt, who flung open the carriage door, ignoring all the rules of etiquette. "Handel is dying!" he cried out to the duke, whom he knew to be a great lover of music and his beloved master's best patron. "I must find a doctor." The duke immediately told him to get into the coach, the horses were given a sharp taste of the whip, and they went to fetch Dr Jenkins from a room in Fleet Street where he was earnestly studying a urine sample. But he immediately drove with Schmidt to Brook Street in his light carriage. "It's all the trouble he's had that's to blame," lamented the secretary despondently as the carriage bowled along. "They've plagued him to death, those damned singers and castrati, the scribblers and the carping critics, the whole wretched crew. Four operas he's written this year to save the theatre, but his rivals hide behind the women and the court, and then they're all mad for that Italian, that accursed castrato, that affected howling monkey. Oh, what have they done to our poor Handel! He's put all his savings into the theatre, £10,000 it was, and now they come plaguing him with their notes of what he owes, hounding him to death. Never has any man done such wonderful work, never has any man given so much of himself, but this would break a giant's back. Oh, what a man! What a genius!" Dr Jenkins, detached and silent, listened.

Before they entered the house he drew on his

pipe once more and knocked out the ashes. "How old is he?"

"Fifty-two," replied Schmidt.

"Not a good age. He's been working like an ox. But he's as strong as an ox too, so let's see what can be done."

The servant held the basin, Christof Schmidt lifted Handel's arm, and the doctor cut into the vein. A jet of blood spurted up, hot, bright-red blood, and next moment a sigh of relief issued from the grimly compressed lips. Handel took a deep breath and opened his eyes. They were still weary, faraway and unaware. The light in them was extinguished.

The doctor bound up his arm. There was not much more that he could do. He was about to stand up when he noticed that Handel's lips were moving. He came closer. Very quietly, it was little more than a breath, Handel croaked: "Over... all over with me... no strength... don't want to live without strength..." Dr Jenkins bent lower. He saw that one eye, the right eye, was staring while the other looked livelier. Experimentally, he raised Handel's right arm. It fell back as if dead. Then he raised the left arm. The left remained in its new position. Now Dr Jenkins knew enough.

When he had left the room Schmidt followed him to the stairs, anxious and distressed. "What is it?"

"Apoplexy. His right side is paralysed."

"And will—" Schmidt hesitated—"will he get better?"

Dr Jenkins ceremoniously took a pinch of snuff. He did not care for such questions.

"Perhaps. Anything is possible."

"But will he remain paralysed?"

"Probably, in default of a miracle."

But Schmidt, who was devoted to his master with every bone in his body, persisted.

"And will he—will he at least be able to work again? He can't live without composing."

Dr Jenkins was already on the stairs.

"No, he will never work again," he said very quietly. "We may be able to save the man, but we have lost the musician. The stroke has affected his brain."

Schmidt stared at him with such terrible despair in his eyes that the doctor himself felt stricken. "As I said," he repeated, "in default of a miracle. Not that I've ever seen one yet."

George Frideric Handel lived for four months, devoid of strength, and strength was life to him. The right half of his body remained dead. He could not walk, he could not write, he could not play a single note on the keyboard with his right hand. He could not speak; his lip hung crooked from the terrible stroke that had torn through his body, and the words that issued from his mouth were only a muted babble. When friends made music for him a little light came into his eyes, and then his heavy, unwieldy body moved like that of a sick man in a dream; he wanted to beat time to the rhythm, but his limbs were frozen in a dreadful rigidity, and his sinews and muscles no longer obeyed him. The once-gigantic man felt helpless, walled up in an invisible tomb. As soon as the music was over his eyelids fell heavily, and he lay there like a corpse once more. Finally the doctor, in despair—for the maestro was obviously incurable—advised sending the patient to the hot baths at Aachen, which might perhaps effect some slight improvement.

But under the frozen exterior, like those mysterious underground hot springs themselves, there lived an incalculable strength: Handel's will, the primeval force of his nature, which had not been touched by the destructive stroke and would not yet allow the immortal part of him to founder in the mortal body. The huge man had not given up, he still wanted to live, to work; and against the laws of nature his will worked a miracle. The doctors in Aachen warned him sternly not to stay in the hot baths for more than three hours at a time; his heart would not survive any longer period, they said, it could kill him. But his will defied death for the sake of life and his burning desire: to recover his health. To the horror of his doctors, Handel spent nine hours a day in the hot baths, and with his will his strength too grew. After a week he could drag himself around again, after a second week he could move his arm, and in a mighty victory of will-power and confidence he tore himself free from the paralysing toils of death to embrace life once again, more warmly, more ardently than ever before, and with that unutterable joy known only to the convalescent.

On the last day before he was to leave Aachen, fully in control of his body, Handel stopped outside the church. He had never been particularly devout, but now, as he climbed to the organ loft with the easy gait so mercifully restored to him, he felt moved by something ineffable. Experimentally, he touched the keys with his left hand. The notes sounded, rang clear and pure through the expectant room. Now he tentatively tried the right hand that had been closed and paralysed so long. And behold, the silver spring of sound leapt out beneath his right hand too. Slowly, he began to play, to improvise, and the great torrent of sound carried him away with it. The masonry of music towered miraculously up, building its way into invisible space, the airy structures of his genius climbed magnificently again, rising without a shadow, insubstantial brightness, resonant light. Down below, anonymous, the nuns and the worshippers listened. They had never heard a mortal man play like that before. And Handel, his head humbly bent, played on and on. He had recovered the language in which he spoke to God, to eternity, to mankind. He could make music, he could compose again. Only now did he feel truly cured.

"I have come back from Hades," said George Frideric Handel proudly, his broad chest swelling, his mighty arms outstretched, to the London doctor who could not but marvel at this medical miracle. And with all his strength, with his berserk appetite for work, the convalescent instantly and with redoubled avidity immersed himself in composition again. The battle-lust of old had returned to the fifty-three-year-old musician. We find him now writing an opera—his right hand, cured, obeys him wonderfully well—a second opera, a third, the great oratorios *Saul* and *Israel in Egypt*, he writes *L'Allegro, il Penseroso ed il Moderato*; his creative desires well inexhaustibly up as if from a long-dammed spring. But the times are against him. The queen's death halts theatrical performances, then the Spanish war begins, crowds assemble daily in the public squares, shouting and singing, but the theatre remains empty and debts mount up. Then comes the hard winter. Such cold falls over London that the Thames freezes over, and sleighs with bells jingling glide over the mirror surface of the ice; all the concert halls are closed at this sad time, for no angelic music dares defy such terrible frosts. Next the singers fall ill, performance after performance must be cancelled; Handel's financial difficulties grow worse and worse. His creditors are dunning him, the critics are scathing, the public remains silent and indifferent, and gradually the desperately struggling composer loses heart. A benefit performance has just saved him from imprisonment for debt, but what a disgrace, to buy back his life as a beggar! Handel becomes more and more reclusive, his mind grows darker and darker. Was it not better to have one side of his body paralysed than his whole soul? In the year 1740 Handel feels a beaten, defeated man once more. His former fame is dust and ashes. Laboriously, he puts together fragments of earlier works, now and then he composes some small, new piece, but the great river of music has dried up; and healthy though his body is again, its primeval force is gone. For the first time that giant of a man feels weary, for the first time the great warrior feels defeated, for the first time he senses the sacred stream of creativity failing and drying up in him, a stream that has flooded a world with music for thirty-five years. Once again he has reached the end, once again. And he knows, or thinks he knows in his despair, that this is the end for ever. Why, he sighs, did God let me rise from my sickbed if men are to bury me once more? It would have been better to die than wander through this empty world in the cold, a shadow of myself.

And in his rage he sometimes murmurs the words of the one who hung on the Cross: "My God, my God, why hast thou forsaken me?"

A lost, a desperate man, weary of himself, doubting his power, perhaps doubting God too, Handel wanders London by night in these months. He does not venture out of the house until late, for during the day his creditors are waiting outside the door to catch him with their notes of his debts, and in the street the glances of scornful and indifferent mankind fill him with disgust. Sometimes he wonders whether to take flight, go to Ireland where they still believe in his fame—but alas, they have no idea how broken his strength is—or to Germany, to Italy; his inner chill might thaw again there, and, touched by the sweet south wind, melody might break from the ravaged rocky landscape of his soul once more. That is the one thing he cannot bear: the inability to create, to compose. He, George Frideric Handel, cannot bear to be defeated. Sometimes he stops outside a church, but he knows that words will not comfort him. Sometimes he sits in a tavern, but a man who has known the high intoxication, the pure and blissful delights of creation feels only repelled by crude distilled spirits. And sometimes he stares down from a bridge over the Thames at the silent river running black as night, and wonders whether it might not be better to cast off all his cares with one determined leap. If only he need no longer bear the burden of this void, the horror of loneliness, forsaken by God and man.

One night he had been wandering in this way again. It was the 21st of August 1741, and the day had been warm and sultry. The sky had weighed down on London as hazy and hot as molten metal, and only when night fell did Handel go for a little fresh air in Green Park. He had been sitting there wearily in the impenetrable shade of the trees, where no one could see him or plague him, for his weariness weighed him down like an illness; he was tired of speaking, writing, playing music, thinking, he was tired of feeling, he was tired of life. Why and for whom should he live? He had gone home, walking like a man drunk along Pall Mall and St James's, urged on by the one compelling idea of sleep: to sleep and know no more, to sleep his fill, for ever if he could. No one was still awake in the house in Brook Street. Slowly—oh, how tired he was, how weary they had made him in hounding him!—slowly he climbed the stairs, their wood creaking at every heavy step he took. At last he was in his study. He struck a spark and lit the candle on the desk; he did it without thinking, automatically, as he had done for years, preparing to set to work. For in the past—and a melancholy sigh involuntarily escaped his lips—he used to come home from every walk with a melody, a theme that he always hastily dashed down so as not to lose the idea in his sleep. But now the desk was empty. No music paper lay on it. The sacred mill-wheel stood still in the frozen mill-stream. There was nothing to begin, nothing to finish. The desk was bare.

Or no: not bare! Wasn't there something white and papery shining in the bright rectangle of light? Handel reached for it. It was a package, and he felt that it contained written papers. He quickly broke the seal. A letter lay on top, a letter from the poet Jennens who had written the libretti for his *Saul* and *Israel in Egypt*. Jennens wrote to say that he was sending Handel a new poem, and he hoped the great genius of music, *phoenix musicae*, would look graciously on his poor words and carry them up on his wings through the ether of immortality.

Handel started as if something terrible had touched him. Did this Jennens too mean to mock him, a dead and crippled man? With a violent movement he tore the letter in two, threw the crumpled remains on the floor and stamped on them. "The blackguard! The scoundrel!" he bellowed; the uncouth fellow had probed his deepest, burning wound and pierced him to the quick, to the bitterest gall of his soul. Angrily he blew out the light, groped his way confusedly to his bedroom and flung himself on the bed; tears suddenly broke from his eyes, and his whole body trembled in the rage of his impotence. Woe to this world, where the robbed are mocked and the suffering tormented! Why appeal to him now that his heart was frozen and the strength had gone out of him, why demand another work from a man whose soul was numbed and whose mind was powerless? All he wanted now was to sleep, unfeeling as a beast, to be forgotten, to be no more! The disturbed, ruined man lay heavily on his bed.

But he could not sleep. There was a restlessness in him, whipped up by his anger like the sea by a storm, a malignant and mysterious restlessness. He tossed from left to right and then from right to left again, becoming ever more wakeful. Perhaps he should get up after all and look at the libretto? But no, what could words still do for him, a dead man? There was no comfort for a man whom God had allowed to fall into the abyss, removing him from the sacred stream of life! And yet a power was still throbbing in him, strangely curious, urging him on, and in his helplessness he could not resist it. Handel rose, went back into his study and once again lit the candle with trembling hands. Had not a miracle raised him once before from the paralysis of his body? Perhaps God knew of healing and comfort for the soul as well. Handel moved the light towards the written sheets of paper. *Messiah*, read the first page. Another oratorio! The latest had failed! But, restless as he was, he turned over the title leaf and began to read.

At the first words he started up. "Comfort ye," began the libretto. "Comfort ye!"—it was like magic, that phrase—no, not a phrase, it was an answer divinely given, the cry of an angel calling from the overcast skies to his despairing heart. "Comfort ye"—how the words resounded, how they shook his subdued soul, those creative, fertile words. Already, although he had hardly read it, hardly sensed it, Handel heard the phrase as music, as hovering, calling, rushing, singing notes. O joy, the gates were flung wide, he could feel and hear in music again.

His hands shook as he turned page after page. Yes, he had been called, summoned, every word entered into him with irresistible force. "Thus saith the Lord"—was that not spoken to him and him alone, was not the same hand that had struck him down now raising him from the earth in bliss? "And he shall purify"—yes, he was purified; all at once the darkness was swept from his heart, brightness had dawned, and the crystalline purity of resonant light. Who had lent such rousing verbal force to the pen of poor Jennens, the poetaster of Gopsall, if not he who alone knew the composer's need? "That they may offer unto the Lord"—aye, a flame of offering had been lit in the smouldering heart, a sacrificial fire leaping to the sky in answer, responding to that magnificent cry. It was spoken to him, to him alone: "Lift up thy voice with strength"—yes, lift it up with the power of the sounding trumpets, the surging chorus, the thunder of the organ, so that once again, as on the first day of creation, the Word, the sacred Logos, might wake mankind, all humanity, all those still despairing in the dark; for truly, "Behold, darkness shall cover the earth", and they know nothing yet of the bliss of redemption granted him in this hour. And no sooner had he read the cry of thanks than the music surged up in him, fully formed: "Wonderful, Counsellor, the Mighty God"—yes, praise him, the Wonderful, the Counsellor who acted to bring peace to the distraught heart! "And lo, the angel of the Lord came upon them"—aye, it had indeed come down into this room on silver pinions, had touched him and redeemed him. How could he not give thanks, rejoice and hail the Lord with a thousand voices in his own, his sole voice, how could he not sing and praise God, saying: "Glory to God in the highest!"

Handel's head was bent over the sheets of paper as if bowed by a stormy wind. All his weariness was gone. He had never before felt his powers so strongly, never before known the joy of creation streaming through him like this. And again and again the words poured over him like torrents of warm, redeeming light, each going straight to his heart, an invocation liberating him. "Rejoice greatly!"—as that magnificent chorus burst forth he involuntarily raised his head and his arms spread wide. "He is the righteous Saviour"—aye, and he, Handel, would bear witness to it as no mortal man ever did before, he would raise his testimony like a shining sign above the world. Only one who has suffered deeply knows joy, only one who has been through tribulations can guess at the ultimate mercy of forgiveness, and it is for him to bear witness to the resurrection before men, for his sake who died. When Handel read the words: "He was despised", sad memories returned to him, transformed into dark, oppressive sound. They had thought he was defeated, they had already buried him alive, hounding him with their mockery—"All they that see him, laugh him to scorn"—yes, they had laughed at the sight of him. "But there was no man, neither found he any to comfort him." No one had helped him, no one had offered comfort in his helplessness, but there came a wonderful power: "He trusted in God", and God had delivered him. "But thou didst not leave his soul in hell." No, God had not left his soul in the tomb of his despair, in the hell of his impotence, a man in bonds, cast out, no, God had called him once again to carry the message of joy to mankind. "Lift up your heads"—how that music broke forth from him now, a great command to proclaim the word of God! And suddenly he shivered, for there, in the hand of poor Jennens, he read: "The Lord gave the word."

He held his breath. Here was the truth, spoken by any chance-come human mouth: the Lord had given him the word; it had come down to him from on high. "The Lord gave the word"; yes, the word was his, the sound was his, the grace was his! And it must go back to God, be raised to him by the overflowing heart; it was every creative artist's duty and desire to sing his praise. Ah, to grasp and hold and raise and wield the word, to draw it out, extend it to the width of the world, embracing all the joy of being, as great as God who gave it—ah, to change the word, the mortal, transient word, back into a thing of eternity through beauty and endless ardour! And behold, there the word was written, there it rang out, a word that could be repeated and transformed for ever: "Hallelujah! Hallelujah! Hallelujah!" Ah, to bring all the voices of this earth together in that word, high and low, the firm voice of a man, the yielding voice of a woman, to make them abundant, enhance them and vary them, bind them and loose them in rhythmical chorus, send them up and down the Jacob's ladder of the scale, soothe them with the sweet sound of strings, rouse them with ringing fanfares, bring them to burst forth in the thunder of the organ: "Hallelujah! Hallelujah! Hallelujah!" Ah, to take that word and that thanksgiving, and make it into jubilation echoing back from this earth and rising to the Creator of the universe!

Tears blurred Handel's eyes, so mighty was the fervour in him. There were pages still to read, the third part of the oratorio. But after that "Hallelujah! Hallelujah!" he could read no more. The words of rejoicing filled his inner being, drew him out, expanding him, burned like liquid fire trying to flow, to stream out of him. And how that jubilation urged him and surged within him, for it wanted to break out, to rise and return to heaven. Hastily, Handel picked up his pen and began setting down notes, forming sign after sign with magical speed. He could not stop, it carried him away like a ship with all sail spread running before a stormy wind. The night around was silent, the humid darkness lay quiet over the great city. But the light poured out within him, and the room echoed, unheard, to the music of the universe.

When his manservant cautiously entered the room next morning, Handel was still sitting at his desk writing. He did not reply when his secretary Christof Schmidt timidly asked whether he could be any help in copying the music, just uttered a low and dangerous growl. No one ventured to approach him again, and he did not leave the study for three weeks. When they brought him food, he hastily broke off a few crumbs of bread with his left hand while the other went on writing. For he could not stop; it was as if some mighty inebriation had seized upon him. When he rose and walked up and down the room, singing aloud and beating time, there was a strange look in his eyes; when anyone spoke to him he started, and his answer was uncertain and confused. Meanwhile, his manservant was not having an easy time. Handel's creditors came demanding payment of his debts, the singers came asking for a festival cantata, messengers came inviting Handel to the royal palace; the servant had to turn them all away, for if he tried to exchange even a word with the composer, who was working so furiously, his incensed master's anger was vented on him like the rage of a lion. George Frideric Handel knew nothing of the time and the hour in those weeks, he made no distinction between day and night, he lived entirely in the sphere that measures time only by musical beat and rhythm, he moved only with the torrents that surged from him ever more wildly, ever more urgently as the work flowed closer to the sacred rapids of its conclusion. Absorbed in himself, he paced up and down the self-appointed dungeon of his study with pounding, rhythmical steps; he sang, he touched the harpsichord, then he sat down again and wrote and wrote until his fingers were sore; never in his life had he felt such surging creativity, never had he lived and suffered like this in music.

At last, after just three weeks—a space of time still incredible today and for all eternity!—at last, on 14th September, the work was finished. The word had become music; what was only dry, sere language before now blossomed and sang, never to fade. The miracle of the will had been worked by the inspired soul, just as the paralysed body had once worked the miracle of resurrection. It was all written down, formed and constructed, rising and unfolding in melody—just one word still remained, the last in the work: "Amen". And now Handel seized upon that "Amen", those two brief, quick syllables, to build them into a stairway of music reaching to the sky. He cast them from voice to voice in alternating chorus, he drew those two syllables out and wrenched them apart again and again, only to merge them anew into yet more ardent sound, and like the breath of God his fervour flowed into that concluding word of his great prayer, so that it was wide as the world and full of its abundance. That one, last word would not let go of him, nor would he let go of it either, building up the "Amen" in a magnificent fugue from the first vowel, the echoing A, the primeval first note, until it was a cathedral, full and resonant, with a spire reaching to the heavens, rising higher and higher, falling again and rising once more, and finally seized upon by the stormy organ, flung up over and over again by the power of the united voices, filling all the spheres, until it was as if the angels themselves joined in that paean of thanksgiving, and the rafters were splintered overhead by that eternal "Amen! Amen! Amen!"

Handel rose to his feet, with difficulty. The pen dropped from his hand. He did not know where he was. He saw nothing, he sensed nothing, all he felt was exhaustion, immense exhaustion. He was so dizzy that he had to lean on the walls. The strength had gone out of him, his body was tired to death, his mind confused. He groped his way along the wall as a blind man might. Then he fell on his bed and slept like the dead.

His manservant knocked softly at the door three times that morning. The maestro was still asleep; his closed face was motionless, as if carved from pale stone. At midday the servant tried to wake him for the fourth time. He cleared his throat noisily, he knocked loudly. But no sound could penetrate the immeasurable depths of that sleep, no word could fall into it. In the afternoon Christof Schmidt came to the servant's aid. Handel still lay motionless. Schmidt bent over the sleeping man, who lay there felled by weariness after his extraordinary feat, like a dead hero on the field of battle after gaining the victory. However, Christof Schmidt and the manservant knew nothing about the great deed and the victory; they felt nothing but alarm to see him lying there so long, so uncannily motionless; they were afraid he might have suffered another stroke. And when, for all their shaking, Handel still would not wake in the evening—he had been lying there sombre and still for seventeen hours—Christof Schmidt went for the doctor again. He did not find him immediately, for Dr Jenkins, making the most of the mild evening, had gone out to fish on the banks of the Thames, and when he was finally tracked down he grumbled about the unwelcome intrusion. Only when he heard that the patient was Handel did he pack up his rod and line, fetch his surgical instruments for the bloodletting that would probably be necessary—all this took a great deal of time—and at last the pony trotted off to Brook Street with the pair of them.

But there was the manservant, waving to them with both arms. "He got up!" he shouted to them across the street. "And now he's eating like six porters. He ate half a Yorkshire ham in no time at all, I've had to pour him four pints of beer, and still he asks for more."

Sure enough, there sat Handel like the Lord of Misrule before a groaning board; and just as he had made up for three weeks' worth of sleep in a night and a day, now he was eating and drinking with all the relish and might of his gigantic body, as if to restore all at once the strength he had put into his work during those three weeks. No sooner did he set eyes on the doctor than he began to laugh, and it gradually became a vast, an echoing, a booming, a hyperbolical laughter; Schmidt couldn't remember seeing a smile on Handel's lips in all those weeks, only strain and anger, but now all the primeval, dammed-up joyousness of his nature burst forth like waves crashing against the rocks, foaming and breaking in rolling sound—never in his life had Handel laughed in so elemental a way as now, when he saw the doctor arriving just as he felt better than ever before, and the lust for life poured roaring through him. He raised his tankard and waved it at the black-clad doctor in greeting. "Devil take me!" cried Dr Jenkins in amazement. "What's come over you? What kind of elixir have you drunk? You're bursting with life! What happened to you?"

Handel looked at him with a smile, his eyes sparkling. Then he sobered down again. Slowly, he rose and went to the harpsichord. He sat down, and at first his hands passed over the keyboard without touching the notes. Then he turned, gave a strange smile, and softly, half speaking and half singing, began the melody of the recitative "Behold, I tell you a mystery"—the words from *Messiah*, and he began them in jest. But as soon as he brought his fingers down through the mild air the music carried him away. In playing, Handel forgot the others and himself as his own current of music swept him gloriously along. Suddenly he was back in the middle of the work, he sang, he played the last choruses which he had written as if in a dream, but now he heard them waking for the first time: "O death, where is thy sting?" He felt the music within him, he was full of the fire of life, and he raised his voice higher, he himself was the rejoicing, jubilant chorus, and on he played and on, singing, all the way to the final "Amen, Amen, Amen". The room was almost shattered by those notes, so forcefully and with such weight did he throw his strength into the music.

Dr Jenkins stood there as if benumbed. And when Handel finally rose the doctor remarked with awkward admiration, just for something to say: "Good heavens, I never heard anything like that before. You must have been possessed by the Devil!"

But at that Handel's face darkened. He too was astonished by the work itself and the grace that had come upon him as if in his sleep. He too felt humbled. He turned away and said so softly that the others could hardly hear it: "No, I think it was God who possessed me."

Several months later two well-dressed gentlemen knocked at the door of the house in Abbey Street, Dublin, at present rented by that distinguished visitor from London the great composer Handel. Respectfully, they put their request: during these last few months Handel had given the capital of Ireland the pleasure of hearing works more wonderful than had ever been performed in the country before. They had heard, they said, that he meant to stage the première of his new oratorio *Messiah* here too; it was no small honour that he did the city in planning to present his latest creation here, even before London heard it, and in view of the extraordinary nature of the concert large profits might be expected. They had come, they said, to ask whether the master, whose generosity was known to one and all, might not donate the takings of that première to the charitable institutions which they had the honour to represent.

Handel looked kindly at them. He loved this city because it had given him its own love, and his heart was open. He would be happy to agree, he said smiling, let them just tell him which institutions were to profit by the performance. "The Society for Relieving Prisoners," said his first visitor, a kindly, white-haired man. "And the sick in Mercer's Hospital," added the other. But of course, they said, this generous donation would be only the proceeds of the very first performance; profits from the others would still go to the master.

However, Handel dismissed this idea. "No," he said quietly, "no money for this work. I will never take money for it, never, I am too much in the debt of another. It shall always go to the sick and the prisoners. For I was sick myself, and it cured me; I was a prisoner and it set me free."

The two men looked up in some surprise. They did not entirely understand. But then they thanked him profusely, bowed, and left to spread the good news in Dublin.

At last, on 7th April 1742, came the final rehearsal. The only audience present consisted of a few relations of the members of the chorus from both cathedrals, and to save money the auditorium of the Music Hall in Fishamble Street was only dimly lit. A couple here, a little group there sat dispersed in isolation around the hall on the empty benches, to hear the new work of the maestro from London; the large auditorium was befogged, dark, cold. But as soon as the choruses began to crash out like great cataracts of sound a strange thing happened. The separate groups involuntarily moved closer together on the benches, gradually forming a single dark block, listening spellbound, for everyone felt as if the unheard-of force of this new music was too much for individuals, as if it would carry them away on its tide. They moved closer and closer as if to listen with a single heart, hearing the confident Word like a single devout congregation, the Word that, spoken and shaped in so many different ways, rang out to them from the intertwining voices. They all felt faint before that primeval strength, yet they were blissfully caught up by it and carried away, and a tremor of delight passed through them all as if through a single body. When the "Hallelujah!" burst out for the first time it brought one man to his feet, and all the others rose too as if at a signal; they felt you could not remain earthbound in the grip of such power, and stood to bring their voices a little nearer to God, offering their veneration in his service. Then they went out to tell the news from door to door: a work of music had been written such as was never heard on earth before. And the whole city was agog with joyful excitement, eager to hear this masterpiece.

Six days later, on the evening of 13th April, a crowd gathered outside the doors of the hall. The ladies had come without hoops in their skirts, the gentlemen wore no swords, so that there would be room for more people; 700, an unprecedented number, crowded in, so fast had the fame of the work preceded it. But not a breath was to be heard when the music began, and the listeners fell very still. Then the choruses burst out with hurricane force, and hearts began to tremble. Handel stood by the organ. He had intended to direct and conduct his work, but it tore itself away from him, he lost himself in it, it became as strange to him as if he had never heard it before, had never made it and given it form, and once again he was carried away on his own torrent. And when the "Amen" was raised at the end his lips unconsciously opened and he sang with the choir, sang as he had never sung in his life before. But then, as soon as the acclamations of the others filled the hall with a roar of sound, he quietly went to one side to thank not the men and women who in turn wished to thank him, but the grace that had given him this work.

The floodgates were opened. The river of music flowed on in him again year after year. From now on nothing could bow Handel, nothing could force the resurrected man to his knees again. Once again the operatic society he had founded in London went bankrupt, once again his creditors came dunning him to pay his debts; but now he stood upright and survived all his trials; undeterred, the sixty-year-old strode on his way, passing the milestones of his compositions. Obstacles stood in his path, but he gloriously overcame them. Old age gradually undermined his strength, weakened his arms, gout afflicted his legs; but undaunted he wrote on and on. At last his eyesight failed; he went blind while he was writing *Jephtha*. But even with blind eyes, like Beethoven with deaf ears, he still wrote on, untiring, invincible, and ever humbler towards God the greater his earthly triumphs were.

Like all true and rigorous artists, he did not praise his own works. But there was one that he loved, *Messiah*, and he loved it out of gratitude because it had saved him from his own abyss, because in it he had redeemed himself. Year after year he performed the work in London, always donating the full proceeds, £500 each time, for the benefit of the Hospital: a man cured to those who were sick, a man set free to those still in bonds. And it was with the work that had brought him out of Hades that he wished to take his own leave. On 6th April 1759, severely ill and now seventy-four years old, he had himself led to the podium of Covent Garden again. There the blind man stood, a huge figure amidst his friends, among the musicians and the singers: with the light gone from his empty eyes he could not see them. But when the surging notes rolled like waves towards him with a great, rushing rhythm, when the rejoicing of certainty rang in his ears, a hurricane swelling from hundreds of voices, his weary face cleared and lit up. He swung his arms in time, he sang as gravely and devoutly with the choir as if he were standing, priest-like, at the head of his own coffin, praying with them for his salvation and the redemption of all. Only once, when the trumpets suddenly came in at the words "The trumpet shall sound", did he start, looking up with his blind eyes as if he were ready now for the Day of Judgement; he knew he had done his work well. He could come before God with his head held high.

Moved, his friends led the blind man home. They too felt it had been a farewell. On his bed, he was still quietly moving his lips. He would like to die on Good Friday, he murmured. The doctors were surprised and did not understand him, for they did not know that this Good Friday would be the 13th of April, the date when the heavy hand had struck him down, the date when his *Messiah* was first performed. On the day when all in him had died, he had risen again. Now he wanted to die on the day when he had risen again, in the certainty of another awakening to life eternal.

And sure enough, his unique will had power over death as well as life. On 13th April Handel's strength left him. He saw nothing now, he heard nothing, his massive body lay on the pillows motionless, a heavy, empty frame. But as the empty seashell echoes to the roaring of the sea, so inaudible music surged within him, stranger and more wonderful than any he had ever heard. Slowly, its urgent swell freed the soul from the weary body, carrying it up into the weightless empyrean, flowing in the flow, eternal music in the eternal sphere. And on the next day, before the Easter bells began to ring, all that had been mortal in George Frideric Handel died at last.

THE GENIUS
OF A NIGHT

―――

THE MARSEILLAISE

―――

25 April 1792

1792. For two months, then three months, the National Assembly of France has been in a state of indecision: should it back war against the coalition of emperors and kings, or should it argue for peace? King Louis XVI himself cannot make up his mind; he has a presentiment of the danger if victory goes to the revolutionaries, he also fears the danger if they are defeated. The various parties are also undecided. The Girondists want war in order to stay in power, Robespierre and the Jacobins champion the cause of peace in order to use the interim period to seize power for themselves. The situation becomes increasingly tense with every passing day, the newspapers wax eloquent, the clubs discuss it all at length, rumours are wilder and wilder, inciting public opinion to become more and more agitated. When a decision does come, therefore, it feels like a kind of liberation. On 20th April, the King of France finally declares war on the Emperor of Austria and the King of Prussia.

An electric, soul-destroying atmosphere has weighed down heavily over Paris during those days and weeks, but even more oppressive and threatening is the sultry mood of agitation seething all along the border. Troops have already assembled in every village, volunteers and members of the National Guard are being equipped in every town, every fortress is put into order, and in Alsace above all they know that, as usual in disputes between France and Germany, the first decision will be taken on Alsatian soil. On the banks of the Rhine the enemy, the adversary, is not such an indistinct emotional and rhetorical concept as in Paris, but part of the visible present perceived by the senses, for you can see the advancing Prussian regiments with your own eyes at the fortified bridgehead and from the cathedral tower. And by night you can hear the enemy's artillery carriages rumbling as they roll along, you can hear weapons clinking, and trumpet signals are blown across the river, which glitters in the moonlight as it flows indifferently on. Everyone knows that only a single word, a single decree is necessary to bring thunder and lightning spewing from the silent mouths of the Prussian cannon, showing that the thousand-year war between France and Germany has broken out again—this time in the name of a new kind of liberty on one side, and to shore up the old order on the other.

THE GENIUS OF A NIGHT

It is a unique day, then, that brings news of the declaration of war from Paris to Strasbourg on 25th April 1792. People immediately stream out of all the streets and houses into the open squares, the whole garrison marches off, regiment by regiment, for its final parade. In the main square Mayor Dietrich awaits them with a sash in the red, white and blue of the tricolour round his waist and the cockade on his hat, which he waves in a greeting to the soldiers. Trumpet fanfares and the beating of drums sound, calling for silence. Raising his voice, Dietrich reads the declaration of war out loud in both French and German, both here and in all the other city squares. After his last words die away, the regimental musicians strike up the first, provisional war song of the Revolution, the *Ça ira*, which is really a sparkling, high-spirited, mocking dance melody, but the thunderous sound of the regiments marching out with their weapons clinking lends it a martial air. Then the crowd disperses, taking the enthusiasm thus whipped up into all the alleyways and houses. Stirring speeches are made in the cafés and clubs, proclamations are made. *Aux armes, citoyens! L'étendard de la guerre est déployé! Le signal est donné!* They begin with these and similar cries, and everywhere, in all speeches and newspapers, on all posters, on all lips, rhythmical phrases are repeated—*Aux armes, citoyens! Qu'ils tremblent donc, les despotes couronnés! Marchons, enfants de la liberté!* Let the crowned despots tremble, such are their exhortations, take up arms, citizens, march on, children of liberty! And every time, the crowd repeats those fiery words with delight.

In the streets and squares, the huge throng is still rejoicing over the declaration of war, but at such moments of public jubilation other voices are also raised, quieter voices that do not entirely agree. Such a declaration also arouses fear and anxiety, but those voices whisper secretly indoors, or keep silent, pale-lipped. There are always mothers saying to themselves: won't the foreign soldiers murder my children? There are peasants in every country anxious for their possessions, their fields, their cottages, their cattle and the harvest. Won't the young seedlings be trampled down, won't their houses be plundered by the brutal hordes, won't blood be spilt in the fields that they cultivate? But the Mayor of Strasbourg, Friedrich Baron Dietrich, who is really an aristocrat, but like the best aristocracy of France at the time is devoted with all his heart to the cause of the new freedom, will let only the loud voices of confidence prevail. He deliberately turns the day of the declaration of war into a public festival. Sash across his chest, he hastens from one assembly to the next, spurring the people on. He has food and wine served to the soldiers as they march away, and that evening, in his spacious house on the Place de Broglie, he assembles the generals, the officers and the most important civil servants for a farewell party, making their enthusiasm seem like a triumphal celebration in advance. The generals, sure of victory as generals always are, preside over the evening, the young officers who see war as the purpose of their lives speak freely. Each encourages his comrades. They brandish their swords, they embrace and drink to one another, and over the good wine they make increasingly passionate speeches. "To arms, citizens! Let us march to save our native land! Those crowned despots will soon tremble! Now that the banner of victory is unfurled, the day has come to spread the tricolour all over the world! Now may every man do his best, for the king, for the flag, for freedom!" Their belief in victory and enthusiasm for the cause of liberty, they think at such moments, will weld the whole nation, the whole country, into a single sacred unit.

Suddenly, in the middle of all the talk and the drinking of toasts, Mayor Dietrich turns to a young captain from the corps garrisoning the fortress, Rouget by name, who is sitting beside him. He has remembered that this amiable officer—not exactly handsome, but likeable—wrote a very nice anthem six months before on the occasion of the proclamation of the constitution. The regimental director of music, Pleyel, set it to music at once. It was not a very demanding work, but had proved easy to sing; the military band had learnt it, it had been sung in choir in the open air of a square. Wouldn't the declaration of war and the march of the departing regiments be the right occasion for a similar celebration? So Mayor Dietrich casually asks, as you might ask a favour of a good friend, whether Captain Rouget (who without the slightest justification has ennobled himself, and is now Captain Rouget de Lisle) whether the captain wouldn't like to mark this patriotic moment by writing something for the troops as they march away, a war song for the army of the Rhine, which is to advance towards the enemy tomorrow?

Rouget, an unassuming, insignificant man who never thought much of himself—his poems have never been printed, his operas have been turned down—knows that occasional verse flows easily from his pen. He expresses himself ready to oblige this distinguished official, who is a good friend of his. Yes, he says, he will try. "Bravo, Rouget," says a general sitting opposite, raising his glass, and telling him to send the work straight after him to the battlefield—the army of the Rhine could do with a good, brisk marching song. Meanwhile another officer is launching into a speech. More toasts are proposed, there is more loud talk, more drinking. General enthusiasm washes like a strong wave over that minor chance exchange between Rouget and the mayor. The mood of the party is ever more ecstatic, louder, more frenetic, and it is some time after midnight when the mayor's guests leave his house.

The hour is late, after midnight. The 25th of April, so exciting a day for Strasbourg with the declaration of war, is over, and it is really the 26th of April now. Nocturnal darkness lies above the houses, but the darkness is illusory, for the city is still in a feverish state. In the barracks, the soldiers are getting ready to march, and behind closed shutters many cautious citizens may already be preparing for flight. A few platoons are marching down the roads, now and then you can hear clattering hooves as dispatch riders pass by, then a rumble again as a battery of heavy artillery comes up, and again and again you hear the monotonous call of the sentries communicating with each other. The enemy is too close, the mind of the city too unsure and agitated for anyone to sleep easily at such a crucial moment.

Rouget, who has now climbed the spiral staircase to his modest little room at 126 Grande Rue, is in a curious state of excitement himself. He has not forgotten his promise to try to write a marching song, a war song for the army of the Rhine, and do it as quickly as possible. He walks restlessly up and down in his small room. How to begin? All the stirring proclamations, the speeches, the toasts are still whirling chaotically around in his mind. "To arms, citizens!... March, children of liberty... we will crush all tyranny! The flag is now unfurled..." He also remembers other words heard in passing, the voices of women trembling for their sons, the peasants' concerns for the fields of France: will they be trampled, will blood be shed by foreign cohorts? Half unconsciously, he writes down the first two lines. They are only an echo, the repetition of the echo, and that cry:

Allons, enfants de la patrie,
Le jour de gloire est arrivé!

Arise, children of this land, the glorious day is here... then he stops and thinks. Yes, that will do. He has the beginning. Now to find the right rhythm, the melody to go with the words. He takes his fiddle out of the cupboard, he tries it. Wonderful: the rhythm fits the words perfectly in the very first bars. He hastily writes on, now carried away by the power that has entered into him. And suddenly it all comes together: all the feelings that are discharged in this hour, all the words that he heard in the street and at the mayor's banquet, hatred of tyrants, fear for his native land, love of liberty. Rouget does not have to compose poetry consciously; all he needs to do is put the words that went from mouth to mouth on this one day into rhyme, set them to the captivating rhythm of his melody, and then he has said and sung everything that the nation felt in its inmost heart. Nor does he have to compose the music deliberately, for the rhythm of the street and the hour comes in through the closed shutters, the rhythm of pride and the challenge in the marching steps of the soldiers, the sounding of the trumpets, the rumble of the cannon. Perhaps he does not hear it himself, not with his own ears, but the genius of the hour that, for this one night, has taken over his mortal frame has heard *him*. And the melody, ever more obediently, goes along with the joyful rhythm that is the heartbeat of a whole nation. As if he were taking dictation from a stranger, Rouget writes down the words and the notes more and more hastily—a storm has broken over him, such a storm as he never felt before in his limited bourgeois mind. It is an exaltation, an enthusiasm that is not his own; instead, a magical force concentrated into a single explosive second carries the poor dilettante 100,000 times beyond his own abilities, and flings him like a rocket up to the stars—a light and radiant flame burning for the space of a second. For one night, it was granted to Lieutenant-Commander Rouget de Lisle to be a brother of the immortals: out of the opening of the song, taken from the street and the newspapers, creative words form at his command and rise into a verse that, in its poetic expression, is as abiding as the melody is immortal.

> *Amour sacré de la patrie,*
> *Conduis, soutiens nos bras vengeurs!*
> *Liberté, liberté chérie,*
> *Combats avec tes défenseurs!*

Love of the fatherland, guide us, support our avenging arms… Then a sixth verse, the last, composed in emotion as a unified whole, combining the words perfectly with the melody, and the immortal song is finished before dawn. Rouget puts out his light and flings himself on the bed. Something, he does not know what, has raised him to a brilliance of the mind that he never felt before, and now something else flings him into dull exhaustion. He sleeps a sleep as deep as death. And the creative spirit, the poet, the genius in him has indeed died. But the completed work lies on the table, now released from the sleeping man, who was truly taken over by that miracle as if in a sacred frenzy. Hardly ever again in the history of all nations has a song so quickly and perfectly been made from words and music.

The same bells ring out from the cathedral to announce the new morning, as usual. Now and then the wind carries the sound of gunfire to the city from the River Rhine; the first skirmishing has begun. Rouget wakes up. With difficulty, he surfaces from a profound slumber. Something has happened, he vaguely feels, something has happened to him, although he has only a hazy memory of it. Only then does he notice the freshly written sheet of paper on the table. Verses? When did I write them? Musical notation in my own handwriting? When did I compose it? Oh yes—the song that my friend Dietrich asked for yesterday, the marching song for the army of the Rhine! Rouget reads his lines of verse, humming the melody that goes with them, but he feels, as the creator of a newly completed work always does, entirely unsure of himself. However, a military comrade is billeted next door to him; he shows his friend the song and sings it. His comrade seems to like it, merely suggesting a few small alterations. This first mark of approval gives Rouget a certain confidence. With all the impatience of an author, and proud to have kept his promise so quickly, he goes straight to the residence of Mayor Dietrich, who is taking a morning walk in his garden and mulling over a new speech. What, Rouget, you mean to say you've done it already? Well, let's have a rehearsal at once. The two of them leave the garden and go into the salon of the house. Dietrich sits down at the piano and plays the accompaniment, Rouget sings the words. Enticed by this unexpected music in the morning, the mayor's wife comes into the room and, trained musician that she is, immediately begins to work on setting the accompaniment so that it can be performed at a party for the friends of the family that evening, along with all kinds of other songs. Mayor Dietrich, proud of his pleasing tenor voice, says he will now study the song more thoroughly, and on the evening of 26th April, the day that saw the composition of its words and music in the early hours of the morning, it is performed for the first time in the salon of the mayor's house to an audience chosen at random.

They seem to have given it a friendly reception, and all kinds of civil compliments were probably paid to the author, who was in the audience himself. But of course the guests in the Hôtel de Broglie on the main square of Strasbourg have not the slightest idea that an eternal melody has descended, on invisible wings, into their earthly present. Contemporaries rarely grasp the true stature of a human being or a musical work on first acquaintance, and we can tell how little the mayoress was aware of that astonishing moment from a letter to her brother, in which she makes the miracle into a banal social event. "You know how many people we receive in this house, and we always have to think of some kind of new entertainment for them. So my husband had the idea of getting a song suitable for the occasion composed. The captain of the engineers' corps, Rouget de Lisle, a charming fellow who writes verse and composes music, swiftly provided the words and notation for a war song. My husband, who has a good tenor voice, sang the piece at once. It is very attractive, and shows certain unique qualities, having the good fortune to be livelier and more spirited than most such songs. For my own part, I turned my talent for orchestration to it, arranging the score for piano and other instruments, which gave me plenty to do. So the piece was played in our house, to the great satisfaction of the whole company."

"To the great satisfaction of the whole company"—that seems to us today surprisingly cool. But the merely friendly impression of mild approval is understandable, for at this first performance the *Marseillaise* cannot display its true force. The song is not a piece for a pleasing tenor voice, to be performed as a solo in a bourgeois salon as part of a programme of romances and Italian arias. It is a song that arouses listeners with the hammering, jaunty, demanding opening bars... *Aux armes, citoyens*...addressing a crowd, a great throng, and its true orchestration is for the clamour of weapons, fanfares blaring, regiments marching. And it is not for the audience at a polite recital, but for those involved, all fighting in the same struggle. It is not to be sung by a single soprano or tenor voice, it is for a crowd of 1,000, the very model of a marching song, a song of victory and death, a song of the singers' native land, the national anthem of an entire nation. The enthusiasm from which it was born will give Rouget's song the power that inspires it. It has not yet taken fire, the melody has not yet reached the nation's soul, the army does not yet know its marching song, its song of victory, the Revolution does not know its eternal paean.

Rouget de Lisle himself, the man who experienced that nocturnal miracle, has as little idea as the others of what he created in a single night, as if sleepwalking and led by a faithless genius. Of course that amiable dilettante is delighted to hear the invited guests applaud his work enthusiastically, to receive their civil compliments as its author. With the petty vanity of a petty mind he industriously tries to exploit this minor success in his small provincial circle. He sings the new tune to his comrades in the coffee houses, he has copies made and sends them to the generals of the Rhine army. Meanwhile, on orders from the mayor and at the recommendation of the military authorities, the regimental band stationed in Strasbourg has studied the *War Song of the Army of the Rhine*, and four days later, when the troops march away, the band of the Strasbourg National Guard plays the new march in the main square. The local Strasbourg publisher patriotically says that he is prepared to print the *Chant de guerre pour l'armée du Rhin*, which is dedicated respectfully to General Luckner by his military subordinates. But not one of the generals of the Rhine army thinks of having the new tune played or sung during the march itself, and so it seems, like all Rouget's efforts to date, that the salon success of *Allons, enfants de la patrie* is destined to remain a one day's wonder, a provincial matter, and as such to be forgotten.

But the innate power of a work cannot be hidden or fade away in the long run. Time can forget a work of art, can forbid it to be performed, leave it for dead and buried, but the elemental will always conquer the ephemeral. For a month, two months, nothing more is heard of the *War Song of the Army of the Rhine*. The printed and handwritten copies lie around or end up here and there, in hands indifferent to it. But if a work has truly aroused enthusiasm in a single human being, that is enough: genuine enthusiasm is creative in itself. At the other end of France, in Marseilles, the Club of Friends of the Constitution gives a banquet on 22nd June in honour of the volunteers marching away to war. Five hundred spirited young men sit at a long table in their new National Guard uniforms, and the atmosphere is as feverish as it was on 25th April in Strasbourg, or indeed even more heated and passionate, thanks to the southern temperament of the people of Marseilles. And now they are not so vain and sure of victory as in that first hour after war was declared. For the war does not live up to the predictions of the generals, who had said that the revolutionary French troops had only to march straight over the Rhine to be welcomed everywhere with open arms. On the contrary, the enemy has made incursions far into French territory. The liberty of France is threatened, the cause of liberty itself in danger.

In the middle of the banquet one of the young men—his name is Mireur, and he is a medical student from Montpellier University—strikes his glass to call for quiet, and gets to his feet. They all fall silent and stare at him, expecting a speech, an address, but instead the young man raises his right arm in the air and strikes up a song, a new song unknown to them all, and no one knows how it came into his hands. *Allons, enfants de la patrie*. And this time the spark catches fire as if it had fallen into a keg of gunpowder. One man's emotion has touched another's; the eternal poles of feeling have come into contact. All these young men, who are setting out in the morning, prepared to fight for freedom and die for their native land, are aware that these words express their innermost will and their own true thoughts. The rhythm irresistibly carries them away into a unanimous ecstasy of enthusiasm. Verse after verse is hailed with jubilation, the whole song must be repeated once, then a second time, and now the melody is their own, they are singing, leaping to their feet in excitement, glasses raised, thundering out the refrain. *Aux armes, citoyens! Formez vos bataillons!* People come in from the street, their curiosity aroused, to hear the song that is being sung with such verve, and then they are singing it too. Next day the melody is on 1,000, 10,000 pairs of lips. A reprint spreads it further afield, and when the 500 volunteers march away on 2nd July the song goes with them. When they feel tired on the road, when their steps slow down, it takes only one man to strike up the anthem again and its irresistible rhythm gives them all new heart. When they march through a village and the peasants gather in amazement, when all the inhabitants assemble to see what is going on, they join in the chorus. It has become their song too. Without knowing that it was meant for the army of the Rhine, without any idea who composed it and when, the volunteers have adopted it as the hymn of their own battalion, bearing witness to their own life and death. It belongs to them, like their regimental banner, and, marching passionately ahead, they plan to carry it all over the world.

The *Marseillaise*—for that will soon be the name given to Rouget's song—wins its first victory in Paris. On 30th July the battalion marches through the suburbs, the banner and the song going ahead of it. Thousands, tens of thousands stand waiting in the streets to give them a festive welcome, and as the men of Marseilles advance, 500 of them singing in time with the song as if it rose from a single throat, singing it over and over again, the crowd listens. What kind of a wonderful, captivating song are the soldiers from Marseilles singing? What fanfare is it that goes to all hearts, accompanied by the beating of drums? *Aux armes, citoyens!* Two hours, three hours later, the refrain is being sung in all the streets of Paris. The *Ça ira* is forgotten, so are the old marches, the worn-out couplets; the Revolution has recognized its own voice, the Revolution has found its song.

It moves on now like an avalanche in a victorious course that cannot be halted. The anthem is sung at banquets, in the theatres and clubs, then even in church after the *Te Deum*, and soon instead of the *Te Deum*. In a couple of months the *Marseillaise* has become the song of the French nation and the whole army. With his clever mind Servan, the first republican Minister of War, recognizes the tonic and exalting power of such a unique battle song. In short order, he gives orders for 100,000 copies to be distributed to all the detachments, and in two or three nights the song of an unknown composer has spread farther than all the works of Molière, Racine and Voltaire. Every party ends with the *Marseillaise*, every battle is preceded by the regimental musicians singing the song of liberty. At Jemappes and Neerwinden the regiments line up to the song for the final onslaught, and the enemy generals, who have no means of stimulating their troops but the old recipe of a double ration of brandy, see in alarm that they have nothing to set against the explosive power of this "terrible" hymn when it is sung by thousands upon thousands at the same time, storming like an echoing wave of sound against their own ranks. The *Marseillaise* now presides over all the battles of France, like Nike the winged goddess of victory, carrying away countless numbers into enthusiastic frenzy and to their deaths.

Meanwhile, an unknown captain of fortifications sits in the little garrison of Hüningen, busily designing ramparts and entrenchments. Perhaps he has already forgotten the *War Song of the Army of the Rhine,* the work he wrote long ago on the night of 26th April 1792, and does not dare to guess, when he reads what the gazettes have to say about that other anthem, the other war song that has taken

Paris by storm, the victorious *Song of the Men of Marseilles*, that it is word for word and bar for bar the miraculous song that came to him and out of him on that night. For by a cruel irony of fate there is only one man who does not feel uplifted by its melody—roaring as it does to the skies, battering against the stars—and that is the man who wrote it. No one in all France troubles about Captain Rouget de Lisle, and the greatest fame that a song ever had is the song's alone; not a trace of it falls on its creator Rouget. His name is not printed on the text, and he himself would remain entirely unnoticed by the masters of the present hour if he had not irritated them by drawing attention to himself. For—a brilliant paradox of the kind that only history can produce—the creator of the revolutionary hymn is not a revolutionary himself; on the contrary, the man who did more than anyone else to promote the Revolution with his immortal song would like to dam it up again as firmly as possible. By the time the men of Marseilles and the Parisian rabble storm the Tuileries and depose the king, with his song on their lips, Rouget de Lisle has had enough of the Revolution. He refuses to take an oath on the Republic, and would rather leave the armed services than serve the Jacobins. The description of *liberté chérie*, beloved freedom, in his hymn is not an empty phrase; he hates the new tyrants and despots in the National Convention no less that he hated the crowned and anointed despots on the enemy side. He frankly vents his dislike of the Committee of Public Safety when his friend Mayor Dietrich, the godfather of the *Marseillaise*, with General Luckner, to whom it was dedicated, and all the officers and aristocrats who were present in the audience on the evening of its first performance, are dragged away to the guillotine. And soon a grotesque situation arises: the poet of the Revolution is imprisoned as a counter-revolutionary, he of all people is put on trial for betraying his native land. Only the 9th of Thermidor, opening the prisons on the fall of Robespierre, spared the French Revolution the shame of having handed over the author of its most immortal song to the "national razor".

However, it would have been a heroic death, and not such a pitiful twilight fate as lies in store for Rouget. For the unlucky man survives the one really creative day of his life by more than forty years, by thousands and thousands of days. He has been stripped of his uniform, his pension goes unpaid; the poems, operas and other texts that he writes are not printed or performed. Fate does not forgive the dilettante for forcing an entrance, unsummoned, into the ranks of the immortals. The little man lives out his little life by dint of working at petty and not always entirely honest businesses. Carnot and later on Bonaparte try in vain to help him. But something in the character of Rouget has been poisoned and distorted beyond redemption by the cruel chance that made him a godlike genius for three hours, and then scornfully cast him back into his own insignificance. He quarrels acrimoniously with all the authorities, he writes audacious and emotional letters to Bonaparte, who wanted to help him; he boasts openly of having voted against him in the constitutional referendum. His business involves him in dubious affairs, and he even becomes an inmate of the Sainte-Pélagie debtors' prison over the matter of an unpaid bill of exchange. Unpopular everywhere, hunted by his debtors, always in bad repute with the police, he finally hides somewhere in the provinces and, as if forgotten and departed in his grave, he listens there to the fate of his immortal song. He still remembers that the *Marseillaise* stormed all the countries of Europe with the victorious armies, that no sooner had Napoleon become emperor than he had it banned from all public musical programmes as being too revolutionary, and then the Bourbons had its performance entirely forbidden. Only with amazement does the embittered old man see how, after an age in human terms, the July revolution of 1830 resurrects his words and melody with their old force at the barricades of Paris, and the Citizen King, Louis-Philippe, grants him a small pension.

It seems to the ruined and forgotten man like a dream that anyone still remembers him at all, but it is not much of a memory, and when he dies at last in 1836 in Choisy-le-Roi, when he is seventy-six, no one knows or can even give his name. Another human age must pass before the *Marseillaise*, by now well established as the national anthem, is sung again in the Great War at the French fronts in warlike conditions, and orders are given for the body of little Captain Rouget to be buried in the same place, the cathedral of Les Invalides, as the mortal remains of little Lieutenant Bonaparte. And so, at last, the creator of a famous song who was never famous himself lies in his native land's place of fame, resting after the disappointment of having been nothing but the poet of a single night.

La Marseillaise

Allons enfants de la patrie,
Le jour de gloire est arrivé!
Contre nous de la tyrannie,
L'étendard sanglant est levé, (bis)
Entendez-vous dans les campagnes
Mugir ces féroces soldats?
Ils viennent jusque dans vos bras
Égorger vos fils,
    vos compagnes!

Arise, children of the fatherland,
The day of glory has arrived!
Against us tyranny
Raises its bloody banner (repeat)
Do you hear, in the countryside,
The roar of those ferocious soldiers?
They're coming right into your arms
To cut the throats of your sons
    and women!

Aux armes, citoyens,
Formez vos bataillons,
Marchons, marchons!
Qu'un sang impur
Abreuve nos sillons!

Que veut cette horde d'esclaves,
De traîtres, de rois conjurés?
Pour qui ces ignobles entraves,
Ces fers dès longtemps préparés?
　(bis)

Français, pour nous, ah!
　　quel outrage
Quels transports il doit exciter!
C'est nous qu'on ose méditer
De rendre à l'antique esclavage!

Aux armes, citoyens…

Quoi! des cohortes étrangères
Feraient la loi dans nos foyers!
Quoi! Ces phalanges mercenaires
Terrasseraient nos fiers
　guerriers! (bis)
Grand Dieu!
　Par des mains enchaînées
Nos fronts sous le joug
　se ploieraient
De vils despotes
　deviendraient
Les maîtres de nos destinées!

To arms, citizens,
Form your battalions,
Let's march, let's march!
Let an impure blood
Water our furrows!

What does this horde of slaves,
Of traitors and conjured kings want?
For whom are these vile chains,
These long-prepared irons?
　(repeat)

Frenchmen, for us, ah!
　　What outrage
What fury it must arouse!
It is us they dare plan
To return to the old slavery!

To arms, citizens…

What! Foreign cohorts
Would make the law in our homes!
What! These mercenary phalanxes
Would strike down our proud
　warriors! (repeat)
Great God!
　By chained hands
Our brows would yield
　under the yoke
Vile despots would have
　themselves
The masters of our destinies!

THE GENIUS OF A NIGHT

Aux armes, citoyens…

Tremblez, tyrans et vous perfides
L'opprobre de tous les partis,
Tremblez! vos projets parricides
Vont enfin recevoir leurs prix!
    (bis)
Tout est soldat pour vous combattre,
S'ils tombent, nos jeunes héros,
La terre en produit de nouveaux,
Contre vous tout prêts à se battre!

Aux armes, citoyens…

Français, en guerriers
    magnanimes,
Portez ou retenez vos coups!
Épargnez ces tristes victimes,
À regret s'armant contre nous.
    (bis)
Mais ces despotes sanguinaires,
Mais ces complices de Bouillé,
Tous ces tigres qui, sans pitié,
Déchirent le sein de leur mère!

Aux armes, citoyens…

Amour sacré de la patrie,
Conduis, soutiens nos bras vengeurs!
Liberté, liberté chérie,
Combats avec tes défenseurs!
    (bis)

To arms, citizens…

Tremble, tyrants and you traitors
The shame of all parties,
Tremble! Your parricidal schemes
Will finally receive their reward!
    (repeat)
Everyone is a soldier to combat you
If they fall, our young heroes,
The earth will produce new ones,
Ready to fight against you!

To arms, citizens…

Frenchmen, as magnanimous
    warriors,
You bear or hold back your blows!
You spare those sorry victims,
Who arm against us with regret.
    (repeat)
But not these bloodthirsty despots,
These accomplices of Bouillé,
All these tigers who, mercilessly,
Rip their mother's breast!

To arms, citizens…

Sacred love of the fatherland,
Lead, support our avenging arms!
Liberty, cherished liberty,
Fight with thy defenders!
    (repeat)

Sous nos drapeaux que la victoire
Accoure à tes mâles accents,
Que tes ennemis expirants
Voient ton triomphe et notre gloire!

Aux armes, citoyens...

Under our flags, shall victory
Hurry to thy manly accents,
That thy expiring enemies,
See thy triumph and our glory!

To arms, citizens...

THE DISCOVERY OF
EL DORADO

J.A. SUTTER, CALIFORNIA

January 1848

A Man Tired of Europe

1834. A steamer bound for America is on its way from Le Havre to New York. In the midst of the desperadoes on board, one among hundreds, is John Augustus Sutter, as he will be known, born Johann August Suter in Rynenberg near Basle in Switzerland. Aged thirty-one, he is in a great hurry to put the seven seas between himself and the European law courts. A bankrupt, thief and forger, he has simply abandoned his wife and three children, has got some money together in Paris with the help of a false passport, and is now off in search of a new life. On 7th July he lands in New York, where he spends two years doing all kinds of possible and indeed impossible jobs, becomes a packer, a pharmacist, a dentist, a medicaments salesman and then a tavern-keeper. Finally, having settled to some extent in the city, he buys an inn, settles down in it, sells it again, and following the magic promptings of the time he moves to Missouri. There he sets up as a farmer, within a short time he owns a little property, and he could live a quiet life. But all manner of people keep passing his house—fur traders, hunters, adventurers and soldiers—they are coming from the west and going to the west, and that word "west" gradually acquires a magical sound. First, everyone knows, you come to prairies—prairies with huge herds of buffalo, you can go for days, for weeks on end without seeing a human soul, apart from the Redskins hunting there; then you reach mountains, high and never yet climbed, and then at last that other land of which no one knows anything for certain except that its fabulous wealth is famous: California, still unexplored. A land flowing with milk and honey, free to everyone who wants to take it—but far away, endlessly far away, and mortally dangerous to reach

But John Augustus Sutter has adventurous blood in his veins, and is not tempted to stay put and cultivate the soil on his holding, however good the soil is. One day in 1837 he sells all his possessions, equips an expedition with wagons and horses and herds of buffalo, and sets out from Fort Independence into the unknown.

The Way to California

1838. Two officers, five missionaries and three women set out in buffalo wagons into the endless void, through prairies and yet more prairies, finally up the mountains and towards the Pacific Ocean. After travelling for three months, they arrive in Fort Vancouver at the end of October. The two officers have left Sutter by then, the missionaries are not going any further, the three women have died of their privations on the way.

Sutter is alone; people try in vain to keep him at Fort Vancouver, offer him a position—he rejects all such suggestions; the lure of the magic name is in his blood.

He begins by crossing the Pacific in a rickety sailing ship to the Sandwich Islands, and after getting into endless difficulties off the coasts of Alaska he lands in a desolate place known as San Francisco. It is not the city of today, which after the earthquake in 1906 has shot up with redoubled growth and has millions of inhabitants—at this time it is a poor fishing village that gets its name from the Franciscan mission; it is not even the capital of the little-known Mexican province of California, lying fallow and desolate without livestock or good growth in the most luxuriant zone of the new continent.

Spanish disorder is made even worse by the absence of any authority, revolts, a shortage of pack animals and human labourers, a shortage of energy to tackle such problems. Sutter hires a horse and takes the animal down into the fertile valley of the Sacramento. A single day is enough to show him that there is not only room for a farm here, indeed for a large estate—there is room for a kingdom. Next day he rides to Monterey, the down-at-heel capital, introduces himself to Governor Alvarado, tells him about his intention of reclaiming the land. He has brought Kanaks with him from the islands, he plans to bring more of those industrious and hard-working indigenous people here regularly; and he takes it upon himself to build settlements and found a small domain called New Helvetia.

"Why New Helvetia?" asks the governor.

"I am a Swiss and a republican," replies Sutter.

"Very well, do as you like. I'll give you a concession for ten years."

Deals, we can conclude, were quickly done there. A thousand miles from any kind of civilization, the energy of a single human being does not carry the same price tag as it does at home.

New Helvetia

1839. A caravan is slowly carting goods along the bank of the Sacramento. Sutter rides ahead on horseback, his gun buckled around him, behind him two or three Europeans, then 150 Kanaks in their short shirts, then thirty buffalo-drawn carts with provisions, seeds and ammunition, fifty horses, seventy-five mules, cows and sheep, then a small rearguard—that is the whole of the army setting out to conquer New Helvetia.

Ahead of them rolls a gigantic wave of fire. They are setting the forests alight as they go along, an easier way of clearing the land than grubbing up the trees. And as soon as the raging flames have swept across the terrain, while the tree stumps are still smoking, they set to work. Storerooms are built, wells dug, seeds sown on soil that needs no ploughing, hurdles are made to pen in the huge flocks and herds. Gradually, more workers arrive from the abandoned mission colonies nearby.

The venture is hugely successful. The seed that has been sown soon yields crops 500 per cent greater than its original quantity. Barns are full to bursting, soon the livestock numbers thousands of animals, and in spite of the local difficulties that are still going on—expeditions against the native inhabitants, who keep making incursions into the flourishing colony—New Helvetia grows to tropically gigantic proportions. Canals are dug, mills and factories built, shipping goes upstream and downstream on the rivers. Sutter supplies not only Fort Vancouver and the Sandwich Islands but also all the ships that put in to the coast of California. He plants fruit, the Californian fruit still so famous and popular today. It does extremely well, so he sends to France and the Rhine for grape vines, and after a few years they cover large areas. He himself builds houses and lays out flourishing farms. He sends to Paris for a piano from the firm of Pleyel—its journey takes 180 days—and to New York for a steam engine, brought right across the continent by sixty buffaloes. He has credits and accounts with the biggest banking houses of England and France, and now, at the age of forty-five, he remembers leaving a wife and three children behind somewhere or other. He writes, inviting them to join him in his principality. For he is aware of all the wealth in his hands: he is the lord of New Helvetia, one of the richest men in the world, and so he intends to remain. At last, moreover, the United States wrests the once-neglected colony from Mexican hands. Now everything is safe and secure. A few more years, and Sutter will be *the* richest man in the world.

A Fateful Cut of the Spade

1848, January. James W. Marshall, his carpenter, suddenly comes bursting into John Augustus Sutter's house in a state of great agitation, saying he absolutely must speak to him. Sutter is surprised; only the day before he had sent Marshall up to Coloma and his farm there to begin work on a new sawmill. And now the man has come back without permission, and stands before Sutter quivering with excitement. He makes Sutter go into his office, closes the door and takes from his pocket a handful of sand with a few yellow grains in it. When he was digging yesterday, he says, he noticed this strange metal, and he thought it was gold, but the other men laughed at him. Sutter takes him seriously; he takes the yellow grains, extracts them from the rest of the sand and tests them. Yes, they are gold. He decides to ride up to the farm with Marshall the very next day, but the carpenter is the first to be infected by the terrible fever that will soon be shaking the whole world. He rides back that night in the middle of a storm, impatient for certainty.

Next morning Colonel Sutter is in Coloma himself. They dam the canal and examine the sand. They have only to take a sieve, shake it back and forth for a little while, and the grains of gold are left shining on the black mesh. Sutter assembles the few white men around him, makes them swear on their word of honour to keep quiet about this find until the sawmill is completed. Then he rides back to his farm in a serious and determined mood. He has matters of great import on his mind: as far as anyone can remember gold has never been so easy to pick up, has never lain in the ground so openly, and that ground is his, it is Sutter's property. A decade seems to have passed overnight, and he *is* the richest man in the world.

The Gold Rush

The richest man in the world? No, the poorest, most wretched and disappointed beggar on this earth. After a week the secret is out. A woman—always a woman, of course!—has told some passing stranger and given him a few specks of gold. And there is no precedent for what happens next. All Sutter's men leave their work, the metalworkers leave the smithy, the shepherds and herdsmen leave their flocks and herds, the wine-growers abandon the vines and the soldiers their guns. As if possessed, they all snatch up sieves and pans in haste and run to the sawmill to sift gold from the sand. Overnight the agricultural land has been abandoned, no one milks the dairy cows, who bellow and die miserably, the herds of buffalo tear down their hurdles and stamp through the fields where the crops are rotting on the stalk, no one is making cheese, the barns are in disrepair, the huge clockwork of the vast enterprise has come to a halt. Telegraphy sprinkles the golden promise over land and sea. And already people are arriving from the cities, from the harbours, sailors leave their ships, government officials leave their posts, they are all coming from east and west in long, endless columns, on foot, on horseback or in carts. It is the gold rush, a swarm of human locusts, the gold-diggers. An aimless, brutal horde knowing no law but the law of the fist, no commandment but that of their revolver, pours over the once-flourishing colony. As far as they are concerned no one owns anything here, and no one dares to resist these desperadoes. They slaughter Sutter's cattle, they tear down the barns to build themselves houses, they trample down the crops in his fields, they steal his machinery—overnight John Augustus Sutter is as poor as a beggar. Like King Midas, he is stifled by his own gold.

And this unprecedented storm in search of gold becomes more and more violent; news of it has reached the outside world, 100 ships set off from New York alone, in 1848, 1849, 1850 and 1851 great hordes of adventurers come over from Germany, Great Britain, France and Spain. Some sail round Cape Horn, but that is too long a journey for the most impatient, who take the more dangerous way across the Isthmus of Panama. A company swiftly decides to build a railway line on the isthmus, and thousands of workers die in the fever of its construction just so that the impatient will be saved three or four weeks and they will get at the gold sooner. Huge caravans cross the continent, people of all races and languages, and they all dig up John Augustus Sutter's property as if it were their own. A city rises in dreamlike haste on the site of San Francisco, which belongs to him by virtue of a signed and sealed governmental act, strangers buy and sell his land to and from one another, and the name of New Helvetia, his domain, disappears behind the magic name of El Dorado, California.

Bankrupt again, John Augustus Sutter stares as if dazed at these enormous seeds of discord that have sprung up. First he tries digging with the others, and even with his servants and companions, to exploit the wealth, but everyone leaves him. So he withdraws entirely from the gold-bearing district, to a remote farm near the mountains, away from that accursed river and the wretched sand, to his farm hermitage. At last his wife and their three grown-up children reach him there, but almost as soon as she arrives she dies of the exhaustion of her journey. But he now has three sons, there are eight arms between them, counting his own; and thus equipped John Augustus Sutter sets to work as an agriculturalist. Once again, but now with his sons, he works his way up, a quiet and tough man making use of the fantastic fertility of the soil. Once again he makes a plan, and he keeps it to himself.

The Trial

1850. California has become one of the United States of America. Under the stern rule of the United States, discipline as well as wealth finally come to that part of the country, obsessed as it is with gold. Anarchy is under control, the laws of the land are enforced again.

And now John Augustus Sutter comes forward with his claims. All the land on which the city of San Francisco has been built, he says, is rightfully his. It is the duty of the state, he says, to make amends for all the damage he has suffered by the theft of his property, and he claims his own part of all the gold taken from its soil. A trial begins, of dimensions never before known to mankind. John Augustus Sutter is taking proceedings against 17,221 farmers who have settled in his own plantations, demanding that they vacate the land they have stolen, and he is asking $25 million compensation from the state of California for simply misappropriating the roads, canals, bridges, dams and mills that he built. In addition he wants another $25 million compensation from the United States as a whole for the destruction of his estates, as well as his share of the gold brought out of the ground. He has sent his eldest son, Emil, to study law in Washington so that he can take proper legal action, and he devotes the enormous income from his new farms to the sole purpose of bringing this expensive lawsuit. He takes it through all the courts for four years.

On 15th March 1855 the courts finally decide on a verdict. The incorruptible judge Thompson, who is the highest legal authority in California, recognizes John Augustus Sutter's rights to the land as fully justified and inviolable.

On that day, John Augustus Sutter has achieved his aim, and he is the richest man in the world.

The End of the Story

The richest man in the world? No, once again the answer is no; he is the poorest and most unfortunate beggar in the world, he is a broken man. When news of the verdict arrives a storm breaks out in San Francisco and its surroundings. Tens of thousands band together, all the people who think they own property but are now under threat, a streetwise mob, a rabble that delights in looting. They break into the Hall of Justice and burn it down, they go in search of the judge, meaning to lynch him, and they set off in a vast throng to plunder all John Augustus Sutter's property. His eldest son, threatened by these bandits, shoots himself; his second son is murdered; the third runs for it but is drowned on the way home. A wave of fire sweeps over New Helvetia, Sutter's farms burn down, his vineyards are trampled underfoot, his furniture, collections and money are stolen and his entire vast property laid waste with pitiless fury. Sutter himself only just escapes with his life.

John Augustus Sutter never recovers from this blow. His work has been destroyed, his wife and children are dead, his mind is confused. Only one idea still flickers faintly in his now-stupefied brain: the law laid down at the trial.

For twenty-five years an old, feeble-minded and poorly dressed man still haunts the Hall of Justice in Washington. The "general" in his grubby overcoat and well-worn shoes, demanding the restitution of his billions, is a familiar figure in all the offices there. And there are always advocates, adventurers and crooks to be found ready to get the last of his pension out of him by persuading him to go to law again. Himself, he does not want money; he hates the gold that has made him poor, has killed his three children and wrecked his life. All he wants is justice, and he defends himself with the querulous embitterment of a monomaniac. He complains to the Senate, he complains to Congress, he puts his trust in all kinds of helpers who, going about the business in just the wrong way, put a ridiculous military uniform on him and drag the unfortunate man as their puppet from office to office, from one set of deputies to another. This goes on for twenty years, from 1860 to 1880, twenty wretched years of beggary. Day after day he wanders around the Capitol, a laughing stock to all the civil servants, mocked by the street urchins—he who owns the richest land on earth, and on whose property the second capital of the gigantic country stands, growing hourly. However, he is left awkwardly waiting. And there, on the steps of Congress, the heart attack that comes as a release strikes him down on the afternoon of 17th June 1880—and a beggar is carried away, dead. A dead beggar, but one with a polemical treatise in his pocket ensuring a claim to the greatest fortune in history to him and his heirs.

No one has ever claimed Sutter's inheritance, no descendant has come forward. San Francisco and all the land around stands on a stranger's property. No one has ever stated the rights of the case, and only one writer, Blaise Cendrars, has at least given John Augustus Sutter what is due to a great fate: the right to be remembered by posterity with admiration.

THE FIRST WORD TO
CROSS THE OCEAN

CYRUS W. FIELD

---

28 July 1858

The New Rhythm

For all the thousands, perhaps hundreds of thousands of years since that strange being known as man has walked the earth, there has been no other maximum degree of human movement than the pace of a horse, of a wheel going round, or of a ship propelled by oars or sails. All the wealth of technical progress within that narrow area illuminated by consciousness that we call the history of the world had yielded no noticeable acceleration in the rhythm of movement. Wallenstein's armies advanced hardly any faster than Caesar's legions; Napoleon's troops were no swifter than the hordes of Genghis Khan; Nelson's corvettes crossed the sea only a little faster than the pirate ships of Viking raiders and Phoenician trading vessels. Lord Byron on his journey as Childe Harold covers no more miles a day than Ovid on his way to exile in Pontus; in the eighteenth century Goethe does not travel in conspicuously more comfort or at greater speed than the Apostle Paul at the beginning of the millennium. Countries lie the same distance from each other in time and space in the age of Napoleon and under the Roman Empire; the resistance of matter still triumphs over the human will.

Only the nineteenth century brings fundamental change to the extent and rhythm of terrestrial speed. In its first and second decades, nations and countries come together faster than for millennia before them. Railways and steamers enable people to cover what were once journeys of many days in a single day, previously endless hours of travel can be completed in time measured by quarters of an hour and minutes. But however much the triumphant new speeds achieved by trains and steamboats are appreciated by contemporaries, such inventions still lie within the sphere of what the mind can grasp. For all these vehicles do, after all, is to multiply previously known speeds five, ten, twenty times over; the outward sight and inner meaning of them can still be followed, and what looks miraculous can be explained. However, the first achievements of electricity, a Hercules still in the cradle, appear entirely unexpected, overturning all earlier laws, smashing all current dimensions. We who were born later will never feel the amazement of that generation faced with the first feats of the electric telegraph, the vast and enthusiastic astonishment on seeing the same small, barely perceptible electric spark—yesterday only just capable of crackling an inch up from a Leiden jar to the knuckle of your finger—suddenly gaining the demonic power to leap across countries, mountains, whole parts of this earth. Or grasping the idea, scarcely thought out yet to its end, that when the ink is still wet on a written word it can be received thousands of miles away in the same second, can be read and understood, and that the invisible current swinging between the two poles of the tiny voltaic pile can be stretched over the whole earth from one end to the other. Or the thought that the apparatus of the physics laboratory, apparently toy-like, that yesterday was just capable of attracting a few shreds of paper if you rubbed a glass plate, can acquire the power of human muscular strength and speed multiplied by millions and billions, carrying messages, moving railway trains, filling streets and buildings with light, and like Ariel hovering invisibly through the air. Only this discovery brought the most crucial readjustment since the creation of the world to the relationship of space and time.

The year 1837—of such significance to the world, when the telegraph made it possible for previously isolated human experiences to be felt simultaneously—is seldom even mentioned in school textbooks, which unfortunately still think it more important to write about the wars and victories of individual nations and military commanders than what are the true triumphs of mankind, because they were achieved jointly. Yet no other date in recent history can be compared with it for the psychological effect of this readjustment of the value of time. The world has changed since it became possible to be in Paris and know simultaneously what is going on in Amsterdam, Moscow, Naples and Lisbon at that very minute. Only one last step has yet to be taken, and then the other parts of the world will also be included in that great connection and a common consciousness of all mankind will be created.

But nature still resists this last unification, still comes up against an obstacle. For another two decades all those countries cut off from each other by the sea will be separated. For a while, thanks to the insulating properties of porcelain, the spark can spring along telegraph poles unimpeded, water sucks up the electric current. But electric wiring cannot be laid through the sea until a means of entirely insulating copper and iron wires has been discovered.

In times of progress, luckily, one invention lends a helping hand to another. A few years after the introduction of telegraph lines on land, gutta-percha is found to be a suitable material for insulating electric cables in water. Now a start can be made on connecting the most important country outside the continent of Europe, Great Britain, to the European telegraph network. An engineer called Brett lays the first cable at the same place where Blériot, later, will be the first to cross the Channel in an airplane. A ridiculous incident intervenes to prevent immediate success: a fisherman in Boulogne, thinking he has found a particularly fat eel, tears the cable out after it has been laid. But on 13th November 1851, the second attempt does succeed. Great Britain is now connected to the Continent, and thus Europe truly becomes Europe, a being that experiences all that is happening with a single brain and a single heart at the same time.

Such a huge success within so few years—for what does a decade mean in the history of mankind?—must naturally arouse boundless courage in the generation that knows it. Everything that you try succeeds, and at dreamlike speed. Only a few years, and Great Britain in turn is connected by telegraph with Ireland, Denmark with Sweden and Corsica with the mainland, and attempts are already being made to connect Egypt and India to the network. One part of the world, however—the most important part—seems doomed to perpetual exclusion from the chain that spans the rest of the world: America. For how can the Atlantic or Pacific Ocean, neither of which has anywhere to stop in its endless breadth, be crossed by a single wire? All factors are still unknown in the infancy of electricity. The depth of the sea has not been plumbed yet, there is only a vague idea of the geological structure of the ocean, and no one has discovered whether a wire laid so deep could stand up to the pressure of so much water above it. And even if it were technically possible to embed so long a cable safely at such depths, where can a ship be found large enough to carry the weight of 2,000 miles of iron and copper cable? Or dynamos powerful enough to send an unbroken electric current over a distance that a steamer would take at least two to three weeks to cross? People of that time lack any relevant assumptions. No one yet knows whether magnetic currents that could divert the electric current circle in the depths of the ocean, no one has good enough insulation, proper measuring apparatus; all that is known so far is the first laws of electricity that have just opened human eyes from their centuries of sleep in oblivion. "Impossible! Absurd!" say scholars, vigorously rejecting the idea as soon as anyone even mentions a plan for telegraphy to span the ocean. "Later, maybe," say the boldest of the technical experts. Such a plan seems a daring exploit with an incalculable outcome even to Morse, the man to whom the electric telegraph owes its greatest perfection so far. But he adds, prophetically, that if the exploit were to succeed, the laying of the transatlantic cable would be regarded as "the great feat of the century".

For a miracle or something miraculous to be perfected, the first step is always the faith of an individual in that miracle. The naïve courage of someone whose mind is closed to reason may give a creative impulse where the learned hesitate to tread, and here, as usual, a simple coincidence sets the grandiose undertaking going. In the year 1854 an English engineer by the name of Gisborne, who wants to lay a cable from New York to the easternmost point of America, Newfoundland, so that news from the ships can be received a few days earlier, has to stop in the middle of his work when his funds run out. So he goes to New York in search of someone to finance him, and there, by pure chance—the father of so many famous things—he meets a young man called Cyrus W. Field, son of a clergyman, who has done so well and so quickly in business that even at a youthful age he could retire to private life with a large fortune if he wanted. At present he follows no profession, but he is too young and too energetic for inactivity in the long run, and Gisborne seeks him out to arouse his interest in laying the cable from New York to Newfoundland. Cyrus W. Field is not—it is tempting to say that luckily he is not—a technologist or any kind of expert. He knows nothing about electricity, he has never seen a cable. But there is a passionate belief in this clergyman's son, the energetic audacity typical of an American. Where the professional engineer Gisborne sees only the immediate aim of connecting New York to Newfoundland, the young enthusiast immediately looks further ahead. Why not connect Newfoundland to Ireland by a cable under the sea next? With an energy determined to overcome all obstacles—he crossed the Atlantic both ways thirty-one times in those years—Cyrus W. Field sets to work at once, firmly intent upon devoting everything in and around him to his purpose, thereby igniting the idea, thanks to which its explosive force becomes reality. The new, wonderful power of electricity has thus allied itself to the other strongest dynamic element of life: the human will. A man has found his life's work, and a task has found the man to carry it out.

Preparation

Cyrus W. Field begins his work with improbable energy. He gets in touch with all the professionals, besieges governments with requests for concessions, leads a campaign in both parts of the world to raise the necessary funds; and so forceful is this entirely unknown man, so impassioned his personal conviction, so powerful his belief in electricity as a new miraculous force, that the equity capital of £350,000 was fully subscribed in Great Britain within a few days. Once the richest businessmen of Liverpool, Manchester and London have come together to found the Telegraph Construction and Maintenance Company, the money streams in. However, the subscribers also include such names as those of Thackeray and Lady Byron, who have no secondary business aim in mind and want to support the work purely out of moral enthusiasm; nothing illustrates the optimistic attitude towards everything technical and mechanical that animated Great Britain in the age of Stephenson, Brunel and the other great engineers as well as the fact that a single appeal is enough to raise such an enormous sum of money for an entirely fantastic venture, from subscribers who cannot be guaranteed that they will recover their investment.

For the enormous expense of laying the cable is all that can be reliably calculated at the beginning of the enterprise. There is no model for the actual technical method of carrying it out. In the nineteenth century, nothing of similar dimensions had ever been devised or planned before. How could spanning an entire ocean be compared with bridging the narrow strip of water between Dover and Calais? There, it had been enough to reel out thirty or forty miles of cable from the deck of an ordinary paddle steamer, and it unwound as easily as an anchor from its winch. And for laying a cable in the English Channel, you could wait for a particularly calm day, you knew the precise depth of the seabed, you were always within sight of one shore or the other and thus not in any danger; the connection could be made comfortably within a single day. But during an ocean crossing of at least three weeks constantly at sea, a reel of cable a hundred times longer and heavier cannot stay exposed on deck to all the rigours of the weather. Furthermore, no ship of the time is large enough to carry that gigantic cocoon of iron, copper and gutta-percha in its hold, or strong enough to carry such a load. Two ships at least will be needed, and these main ships must in turn be accompanied by others so that they can keep precisely to the shortest course and have help ready to hand in the case of any accident. It is true that the British government has made the *Agamemnon* available for this venture— one of its largest warships, a vessel that fought off Sebastopol—and the American government had contributed the *Niagara*, a frigate of 5,000 tons, the largest possible at the time. However, both ships must be specially converted first, so that each can carry half of the endless chain intended to link two parts of the world with each other. But the main problem remains the cable itself. That gigantic umbilical cord between two parts of this earth is exposed to unimaginable stress. For one thing, the cable must be as strong and resistant as a steel rope, and at the same time elastic enough to be easily paid out. It must stand up to any pressure and any strain, and yet be as easy to tie off smoothly as a silk thread. It must be massive, yet not take up too much space; it must be solid, yet sensitive enough to let the slightest electric wave pass along it for 2,000 miles. The smallest tear in it, the least unevenness at any single part of this gigantic cable can wreck it on its fourteen-day journey.

But the venture is made. Factories are at work day and night, all the cogwheels drive that one man's demonic will forward. Whole mines of iron and copper are needed for this one cable, whole forests of rubber trees must be tapped to make the gutta-percha insulation to cover such a great distance. And nothing more vividly illustrates the enormous proportions of the enterprise than the fact that 367,000 miles of a single wire are spun into this one cable, thirteen times as much as would go around the entire earth, and enough to connect the earth with the moon in a single line. Not since the building of the Tower of Babel has mankind ventured anything more technically magnificent.

The First Start

The machinery whirrs for a year, wire reels out from the factories into both ships all the time like a thin, flowing thread, and at last, after thousands and thousands of revolutions, half the cable is rolled up in a spool on each of the ships. The new, cumbersome engines have also been built and installed; provided with brakes and a reverse gear, they are to lower the cable to the depths of the ocean in an uninterrupted process taking one, two or three weeks. The best electricians and technical experts, including Morse himself, have assembled on board in order to keep an eye on their apparatus and check it while the cable is being laid to make sure that there is no break in the electric current. Reporters and artists have joined the fleet as well to describe this voyage, the most exciting since the days of Columbus and Magellan in words and pictures.

At last everything is ready for the ships to leave, and although hitherto sceptics have been in the majority, the public interest of Great Britain as a whole now turns to passionate enthusiasm for the venture. On 5th August 1857, hundreds of small boats and ships are circling around the fleet carrying the cable in the little Irish harbour of Valentia to take part in the historic moment when one end of the cable is carried to the coast by boats and made fast on the mainland of Europe. The departure of the ships becomes a solemn occasion. The government has sent representatives, and in a moving address a priest prays for God's blessing on the bold venture. "O Eternal God," he begins, "Thou who hast spread out the heavens and mastered the surging of the sea, Thou whom the winds and the waves obey, in Thy mercy look down on Thy servants... hold sway over every obstacle, remove all resistance that might prevent us from carrying out the performance of this great work." And then thousands of hands wave and thousands of hats are raised from the shore and the sea. Slowly, the land disappears. An attempt is being made to realize one of mankind's boldest dreams.

A Misfortune

The original plan had been for the two great ships, the *Agamemnon* and the *Niagara*, each carrying half the cable, to arrive with each other at a point in the middle of the ocean, calculated in advance, and only there would the two halves be riveted together. Then one ship was to steer west for Newfoundland, the other east to Ireland. But it seemed too audacious to venture so much expensive cable at the first attempt, so it was decided, instead, to lay the first part of the line from the mainland while no one yet knew for certain whether telegraphic transmission beneath the sea worked properly at all over such distances.

Of the two vessels, the task of laying the cable from the mainland to the middle of the sea is given to the *Niagara*. Slowly and cautiously, the American frigate steers a course to that point, all the time leaving the thread of the cable behind like a spider spinning silk from its huge body. Slowly and regularly, the engine laying the cable rattles on board the ship—it is the sound well known to all seamen of an anchor cable being paid out as it unreels from the winch. After a few hours the men on board pay no more attention to the regular grinding sound than they do to their own heartbeats.

Further and further out to sea, always lowering the cable into the water behind the keel. This adventure seems far from adventurous. Only the electricians sit in a special room listening, constantly exchanging signals with the Irish mainland. And, wonderful to relate, although the coast has long ago been out of sight, transmission along the underwater cable is as clear as if one European city were communicating with another. They have already left the shallow waters behind, they are part of the way over what is known as the deep-sea plateau that rises beyond Ireland, and still the metal thread is running regularly down behind the keel like sand in an hourglass, sending and receiving messages at the same time.

Three hundred and thirty-five miles of cable have already been laid, more than ten times the distance from Dover to Calais; five days and five nights of initial uncertainty have already passed, and on the sixth evening, on 11th August, Cyrus W. Field is going to bed after many hours of work and stress to get some well-earned rest. Then, suddenly—what has happened?—the rattling sound stops. And just as someone sleeping in a moving train starts up when the locomotive unexpectedly stops, just as the miller wakes in his bed when the mill-wheel suddenly stops going round, so all on board the ship are instantly awake and running up on deck. A first glance at the engine shows that the reel running out is empty. The cable has suddenly slipped off the winch, it was impossible to catch the end that came away in time, and now it is even more impossible to find the lost end in the depths and bring it up again. A terrible thing has happened. A small technical fault has wrecked the work of years. The men who set out so boldly return, defeated, to Great Britain, where the sudden silencing of all signals has already paved the way for bad news.

Misfortune Again

Cyrus Field, the only imperturbable man involved, hero and businessman both, takes stock. What has been lost? Three hundred miles of cable, £100,000 of share capital, and—what troubles him even more—a whole irreplaceable year. For the expedition can hope for good weather only in summer, and this year the season is already too far advanced to try again. On the other side of the account that Field is drawing up, there is a small profit: a great deal of practical experience has been gained in this first attempt. The cable itself, having proved its worth, can be wound up and put away ready for the next expedition. Only the engines for laying the cable, which were to blame for the fateful break in it, must be altered.

So another year passes in waiting and preparatory work. Not until 10th June 1858 can the same ships set out again, with a cargo of new courage and the old cable. As the electrical transmission of signals worked perfectly on the first voyage, Field and the others have returned to the old plan of beginning to lay cables out on both sides from the middle of the ocean. The first few days of the second voyage pass without incident. Only on the seventh day is the laying of the cable, and thus the real work, to begin at the place calculated in advance. Up to this point everything is, or seems to be, a pleasure cruise. The engines are not in use, the sailors can rest and enjoy the fine weather, the sky is cloudless and the water still—perhaps too still.

On the third day, however, the captain of the *Agamemnon* feels secretly uneasy. A glance at the barometer has shown him how alarmingly fast the quicksilver column is falling. A storm of an unusual kind must be brewing, and sure enough a storm does break on the fourth day, such a storm as even the most experienced seamen on the Atlantic Ocean have seldom seen. This hurricane strikes the British cable-laying ship, the *Agamemnon*, with fatal severity. In itself an excellent vessel that has withstood the harshest trials in all seas and even in war, the flagship of the British Navy ought to be able to withstand this terrible storm as well. But unfortunately the ship has been entirely converted for laying the cables in order to accommodate such a huge weight. This is not like a freighter, where the weight can be equally distributed on all sides of the hold; the whole weight of the gigantic spool lies in the middle, and only part of it is entirely in the foreship, with the even worse result that every time the ship goes up and down in rough seas that part of the ship swings back and forth with redoubled force. That means that the storm can play a dangerous game with its victim: the ship is raised forward and backward up to an angle of forty-five degrees, breakers flood down on the deck, any objects not lashed down there are smashed. Then there is another misfortune—in the worst of the storm, when the ship is shaken from the keel to the mast, the shed containing the cargo of coal heaped on deck gives way. The whole mass comes down like a storm of black hail over the sailors, who are already bleeding and exhausted. Some are injured by their fall, others scalded as pans tip over in the galley. One sailor goes mad in the ten-day storm, and the crew are already thinking of the desperate measure of throwing part of the fateful cable overboard. Fortunately the captain refuses to take the responsibility for that, and he is right. The *Agamemnon* survives the ten days of storm, after unspeakable travails, and although badly delayed manages to join the other vessels at the place in the ocean where the laying of the cable was to begin.

Only now, however, is it clear how much the valuable and sensitive cargo of wires has suffered, entangled thousands of times as it was flung back and forth in heavy seas. The separate wires are intertwined in many places, their gutta-percha covering is rubbed or torn. Without much confidence, they make a few attempts to lay the cable all the same, but the only result is the loss of some

200 miles of cable that disappear uselessly into the sea. For the second time the voyage has to be abandoned, and they go home, not in triumph but crestfallen.

The Third Voyage

Pale-faced and already aware of the bad news, the shareholders in London are waiting for their leader—and the man who tempted them into the venture—Cyrus W. Field. Half of the share capital has been lost on those two voyages, and nothing has been proved, nothing achieved. It is understandable that most of them now feel enough has been done. The chairman advises salvaging what can still be salvaged. He is in favour of bringing what remains of the cable back from the ships and selling it, if necessary even at a loss, before drawing a line under that wild plan to stretch a telegraph line under the ocean. The deputy chairman closes ranks with him and sends notice of his resignation in writing, to demonstrate that he wants no more to do with the absurd enterprise. But there is no shaking the tenacity and idealism of Cyrus W. Field. Nothing is lost, he explains. The cable itself passed the test with flying colours, and there is still enough on board to make a new attempt; the fleet is assembled, the crews hired. The very fact that there was such an unusual storm last time suggests that the ships can hope for a period of fine, calm weather now. Courage, he says, take heart again! Now or never is the opportunity to dare the ultimate venture.

The shareholders look at one another more and more uncertainly: are they to entrust the last of the capital they paid into the scheme to this fool? But as a strong will will always finally sweep the hesitant away with it, Cyrus W. Field forces the others to decide on another voyage. On 17th July 1858, five weeks after the last, disastrous voyage, the fleet leaves its British harbour for the third time.

And now the truth of the old adage that crucial matters almost always succeed in secret is confirmed. This time there are no observers of the departure; no boats large or small circle round the ships wishing them luck, no crowd gathers on the beach, no festive dinner is held, no speech is made, no priest calls on God to be with the enterprise. The ships put out to sea, surreptitiously and in silence. But a kindly sea awaits them. Precisely on the day agreed, 28th July, eleven days after the departure from Queenstown, the *Agamemnon* and the *Niagara* are able to begin their great task at the appointed place in the middle of the ocean.

It is a strange sight. The ships turn to each other, stern to stern. The ends of the cable are riveted together between them. Without any formality—and even the men on board, tired as they are of unsuccessful attempts, watch with little interest—the iron and copper cable sinks down between the two ships to the bottom of the sea, unplumbed as yet by any lead-line. There is one more greeting from deck to deck, flag to flag, and the British ship steers for Britain, the American ship for America. While they move away from each other, two wandering points in the endless ocean, the cable constantly holds them together—and for the first time in human history two ships can communicate with each other beyond wind and water, space and distance, now invisible to one another. Every few hours one of the vessels sends an electric signal from the depths of the ocean recording the number of miles it has travelled, and every time the other ship confirms that, thanks to the good weather, she too has gone the same distance. A day passes like this, and then another, a third, a fourth. At last, on 5th August, the *Niagara* is able to report its arrival in Trinity Bay, Newfoundland, and can see the American coast ahead, after laying no less than 1,030 miles of cable. The *Agamemnon* is likewise triumphant, having also embedded about 1,000 miles securely in the depths, and the British ship has the Irish coast in sight. But only those two ships, those few hundred men in their wooden accommodation, know that the deed has been done.

The world is not aware of it yet, having forgotten the venture long ago. No one is waiting for them on the beach in Newfoundland or Ireland—but in that single second when the new cable under the ocean joins the cable on land, the whole of mankind will know of their great joint victory.

The Great Hosanna

It is for the very reason that this lightning flash of joy strikes out of a clear blue sky that it burns so brightly. The old and the new continents receive news of the project's success at almost the same hour early in August. The effect is indescribable. *The Times*, usually thoughtful and measured in its pronouncements, says in a leading article: "Since the discovery of Columbus, nothing has been done in any degree comparable to the vast enlargement which has thus been given to the sphere of human activity." The City is in a state of great excitement. But the pride and delight felt in Great Britain is restrained and muted by comparison with the hurricane of enthusiasm in America as soon as the news breaks there. Business grinds to a halt, the streets are crowded with people asking questions and deep in loud discussion. A complete unknown, Cyrus W. Field, has become the hero of an entire nation overnight. He is placed firmly beside Franklin and Columbus; the whole of New York and a hundred more cities are agog with expectation to see the man whose determination has brought about "the marriage of young America and the Old World". But the enthusiasm has not yet reached its highest point; for the time being, there is nothing to go on but the dry announcement that the cable has been laid. However, can it speak as well? Has the achievement really succeeded? It is a great spectacle—an entire city, an entire country is waiting and listening for a single word, the first word to cross the ocean. Everyone knows that the Queen of England will be first to send a message of congratulation, and it is expected ever more impatiently hour by hour. But days and days pass, because by unlucky chance the cable to Newfoundland has been destroyed, and it is not until 16th August that the message from Queen Victoria reaches New York in the evening.

The much-desired news arrives too late for the papers to print the official information; only a summary can be delivered to the telegraph and newspaper offices, and at once huge crowds gather. Newspaper boys have to make their way through the turmoil dishevelled, their clothes torn. The news is announced in the city's restaurants and theatres. Thousands who cannot yet grasp the fact that a telegraph message can arrive many days ahead of the fastest ship run down to the harbour in Brooklyn to welcome the heroic ship responsible for this peaceful victory, the *Niagara*. Next day, 17th August, the newspapers rejoice in headlines as thick as a finger: "The cable in perfect working order", "Everybody crazy with joy", "Tremendous sensation throughout the city", "Now's the time for an universal jubilee". It is an unheard-of sensation: for the first time since thinking began on earth, a thought has crossed the ocean in the time it took to think it. And already 100 cannon shots are thundering out from the Battery to announce that the President of the United States has replied to the Queen. No one dares to doubt now; that evening New York and all the other cities are radiant with tens of thousands of lights and torches. Every window is illuminated, and the fact that the dome of City Hall burns down hardly disturbs the joyful celebrations. For the very next day brings new rejoicings: the *Niagara* has arrived; the great hero Cyrus W. Field is there! The rest of the cable is carried through the city in triumph, and the ship's crew is fêted. Such manifestations are repeated daily in every city from the Pacific Ocean to the Gulf of Mexico, as if America were celebrating its discovery for the second time.

Yet still that is not enough! The real triumphal

procession is to be even more ostentatious, the finest the New World has ever seen. The preparations take two weeks, and then, on 31st August, a whole city celebrates the work of a single man, Cyrus W. Field, as hardly any victor since the days of the Caesars and the emperors has ever been applauded by his people. A festive procession is made ready on that fine autumn day, so long a procession that it takes six hours to go from one end of the city to the other. Regiments march ahead with banners through streets lined by flags, followed in an endless line by wind bands, singing groups and societies, the fire brigade, the schools and the veterans. Everyone who can march does, everyone who can sing does, everyone who can rejoice rejoices. Cyrus W. Field is driven through the city in a carriage and four, like an emperor of antiquity celebrating his triumph, with the captain of the *Niagara* in another and the President of the United States in a third, with the mayor, the officials and the professors following behind. There are endless speeches, banquets, torchlight processions, the church bells peal, the cannon thunder, and again and again rejoicing surrounds the new Columbus who has united the two worlds, the conqueror of space, the man who in this hour has become the most famous and idolized man in America, Cyrus W. Field.

Crucify Him!

Thousands, millions of voices are shouting in jubilation that day. Only one voice, the most important, remains strangely silent during the celebrations—the voice of the electric telegraph. In the midst of the rejoicing, perhaps Cyrus W. Field guesses the terrible truth, and it must have been appalling for him to be the only one who knew that on that very day the Atlantic cable has stopped working after, in the last few days, increasingly confused and barely legible signals had come in. Finally the wire has drawn its last, dying breath. In all America no one knows or guesses at the gradual failure, apart from the few who control the reception of transmissions in Newfoundland, and even they, in view of the unbounded rejoicing, hesitate for several days to pass on the bitter information to the jubilant crowds. Soon, however, people begin to notice the paucity of incoming messages. America had expected that now news would be flashing over the ocean every hour—instead, there is only, from time to time, a vague announcement that cannot be checked. It is not long before a rumour is being whispered: in enthusiasm and impatience to achieve better transmissions, over-strong electrical charges have been sent along the line, thus entirely wrecking the cable that was inadequate anyway. They still hope to put things right, but soon there is no denying that the signals are getting more indistinct and less and less comprehensible. Just after that wretched morning following the festivities, on 1st September, clear tones and distinct vibrations stop crossing the sea entirely.

There is nothing that human beings are less likely to forgive than being brought down to earth in the middle of genuinely felt enthusiasm, and seeing themselves disappointed behind their backs by a man of whom they expect everything. As soon as the rumour that the much-famed telegraph has failed is proved true, the stormy current of jubilation turns to a reverse wave of vicious embitterment breaking over Cyrus W. Field, the innocently guilty party. He has deceived a city, a country, the whole world; they are saying in the City of London that he knew about the failure of the telegraph long before it happened, but selfishly let himself enjoy the adulation while he used the time to sell his own shares at a huge profit. There are even more vicious accusations, including the strangest of all, the peremptory claim that the Atlantic telegraph never worked properly; everything said about it was deception and humbug, and the telegram from Queen Victoria had been written in advance and never came over the oceanic telegraph line. Not a single message, says this rumour, really came across the seas in comprehensible form all that time, and the directors of the company simply thought up imaginary messages consisting of assumptions and fragmentary signals. A positive scandal breaks out. Those who were most jubilant yesterday are the most indignant now. An entire city, an entire country is ashamed of its overheated and over-hasty enthusiasm. Cyrus W. Field becomes the victim of this fury; only yesterday still a national hero, regarded as the brother of Franklin and in the line of descent from Columbus, he has to hide like a malefactor from his former friends and admirers. A single day made his fame, a single day has destroyed it. The ill effects cannot be foreseen, the capital is lost, confidence is gone; and, like the legendary serpent of Midgard, the useless cable lies in the unseen depths of the ocean.

Six Years of Silence

The forgotten cable lies useless in the ocean for six years; for six years the old, cold silence lords it once again over the two continents that, for a brief time, sent pulsating signals to each other. Two continents that had been as close as a breath once drawn, as close as a few hundred words, America and Europe are separated, as they have been for millennia, by insuperable distance. The boldest plan of the nineteenth century, only yesterday almost reality, has become a legend once more, a myth. Of course no one thinks of returning to the project that half succeeded; the terrible defeat has crippled all their powers and stifled all their enthusiasm. In America the civil war between the north and the south diverts all attention from other questions; in Great Britain committees still meet now and then, but it takes them two years to come to the arid conclusion that, in principle, a cable running under the sea would be possible. But the path from academic theory to application of the principle is not one that anyone thinks of treading. For six years, all work on the project lies as much at rest as the forgotten cable at the bottom of the sea.

However, while six years are only a fleeting moment within the huge space of history, they mean as much as a thousand in so young a science as electricity. Every year, every month brings new discoveries in that field. Dynamos become stronger and stronger, more and more precise, have more and more applications, the functioning of electrical apparatus is ever more exact. The telegraph network already spans the internal areas of all the continents; it has already crossed the Mediterranean and linked Africa and Europe. So as year follows year the idea of crossing the Atlantic Ocean imperceptibly comes to lose more and more of the fantastic aura that has clung to it for so long. The time when the attempt is made again is bound to come inexorably closer. All that is missing is the man to infuse new energy into the old plan.

And suddenly the man is there—and lo and behold, he is the same man as before, with the same faith and confidence in the idea: Cyrus W. Field, resurrected from the exile of silence and malicious scorn. He has crossed the ocean for the thirtieth time and returns to London; he succeeds in providing new capital of £600,000 for the old concessions. And at last the giant ship he has dreamt of so long is also available, a vessel that can carry the enormous freight on its own, the famous *Great Eastern*, with its 22,000 tons and four funnels, built by Isambard Kingdom Brunel. Furthermore, wonderful to relate, it is not in use this year because, like the undersea cable project itself, it is ahead of its time. It can be bought and equipped for the expedition within two days.

Now everything that was once immeasurably difficult is easy. The mammoth ship, carrying a new cable, leaves the Thames on 23rd July 1865. Although the first attempt fails because of a tear in the cable two days before the laying is completed, and the insatiable ocean swallows up £600,000 sterling, technology is now too sure of itself to be discouraged. And when the *Great Eastern* sets out for the second time on 13th July 1866, the voyage is a triumph. This time the cable calls back to Europe clearly and distinctly. A few days later the old, lost cable is found, and two strands of cable now link the Old and New Worlds into one. What was miraculous yesterday is taken for granted today, and from that moment on the earth has, so to speak, a single heartbeat. Mankind now lives able to hear, see and understand itself simultaneously from one end of the earth to the other, made divinely omnipresent by its own creative power. And, thanks to its victory over space and time, mankind would be united for ever, if it were not confused again and again by the fateful delusion constantly destroying that grandiose union, enabling it to destroy itself by the same means that give it power over the elements.

Also available

TRIUMPH AND DISASTER

—

FIVE HISTORICAL MINIATURES

—

STEFAN ZWEIG

Pushkin Press

Pushkin Press was founded in 1997, and publishes novels, essays, memoirs, children's books—everything from timeless classics to the urgent and contemporary.

Our books represent exciting, high-quality writing from around the world: we publish some of the twentieth century's most widely acclaimed, brilliant authors such as Stefan Zweig, Marcel Aymé, Teffi, Antal Szerb, Gaito Gazdanov and Yasushi Inoue, as well as compelling and award-winning contemporary writers, including Andrés Neuman, Edith Pearlman, Eka Kurniawan and Ayelet Gundar-Goshen.

Pushkin Press publishes the world's best stories, to be read and read again. Here are just some of the titles from our long and varied list. To discover more, visit www.pushkinpress.com.